Should We Ban
Killer Robots?

Political Theory Today

Deane Baker

Should We Ban
Killer Robots?

polity

First published in 2022 by Polity Press

Polity Press
65 Bridge Street
Cambridge CB2 1UR, UK

Polity Press
101 Station Landing
Suite 300
Medford, MA 02155, USA

ISBN-13: 978-1-5095-4850-7
ISBN-13: 978-1-5095-4851-4 (pb)

A catalogue record for this book is available from the British Library.

Library of Congress Control Number: 2021942477

Typeset in 11 on 15pt Sabon
by Cheshire Typesetting Ltd, Cuddington, Cheshire
Printed and bound in Great Britain by TJ Books Ltd, Padstow, Cornwall

For further information on Polity, visit our website:
politybooks.com

Contents

Acknowledgements

I am grateful to have had the opportunity to trial earlier versions of several of the arguments in this book in other forums. Parts of what follows first appeared in 'Autonomous Weapons and the Epistemology of Targeting', in the Defence-in-Depth blog (10 September 2018), 'The Awkwardness of the Dignity Objection to Autonomous Weapons', in the *Strategy Bridge* journal (6 December 2018) and 'The Robot Dogs of War', in Jai Galliott, Duncan MacIntosh and David Ohlin (eds), *Lethal Autonomous Weapons: Re-examining the Law and Ethics of Robotic Warfare* (Oxford University Press 2021). I have also drawn on arguments that appeared in my books *Just Warriors, Inc.: The Ethics of Privatised Force* (Continuum 2010) and *Citizen Killings: Liberalism, State Policy and Moral Risk* (Bloomsbury Academic 2016). Along the way I have received insightful inputs from friends, students and colleagues, including Liran Antebi, Ned Dobos, Erin Hahn, Mark Hilborne, David Kilcullen, Peter Lee, Rain Liivoja, Ian MacLeod, Rob McLaughlin, Valerie Morkevicius, David Pfotenhauer, Shashank Reddy, Julian Tattersall and Mathew Wann (among others). I am particularly grateful for comments on the final draft by the two anonymous readers and for the guidance of George Owers and the team at Polity.

This book is dedicated to my daughters, the fabulous Baker girls: Jemimah, Kezi and Amelia.

Introduction

If you haven't yet watched the short film *Slaughterbots* on YouTube, you really should do so now. I mean it – stop reading immediately and watch the video before going any further. You won't regret it, *Slaughterbots* is short and impressively well executed. Besides, what I say below contains spoilers.

Slaughterbots was created by the Future of Life Institute in conjunction with Stuart Russell from the University of California at Berkeley. The film garnered over 350,000 views on YouTube in the first four days after its release, and was reported on by a large range of news outlets, from CNN to the *Telegraph*. The fictional near-future scenario depicted in this film in vivid Hollywood thriller style is both entertaining and scary, but is scripted with serious intent. As Russell explains at the end of the video, *Slaughterbots* is intended to help us see that, while AI's 'potential to benefit humanity is enormous, even in defence', we must nonetheless draw a line. Ominously, he warns us that 'the window to act is closing fast'. The key issue is that '[a]llowing machines to choose to kill humans will be devastating to our security and our freedom' (Sugg 2017).

The film opens with a Steve Jobs-like figure speaking on stage at the release of a new product. Only, instead of the next generation of iPhone, the product is a weapon – a tiny autonomous quadcopter loaded with three grams of shaped explosives, and which combines artificial intelligence (AI) and facial recognition technology to lethal effect. After proudly explaining that 'its processor can react 100 times faster than a human', the Steve Jobs of Death demonstrates his creation. We watch as he throws it into the air, and it then buzzes autonomously, like an angry hornet, over to its designated target – in this case a humanoid dummy. After latching parasitically onto the forehead of this simulated enemy soldier, the drone fires its charge, neatly and precisely destroying the simulated brain within, to the applause of the adoring crowd. If that were not demonstration enough, a video then plays on the giant screen, showing a group of men in black fatigues in an underground car park. The mosquito-like buzzing of the quadcopter causes the men to scatter in fear, only to be killed one by one as the tiny drones identify, track and engage them, detonating their charges with firecracker-like pops. 'Now *that* is an airstrike of surgical precision', says Mr Death-Jobs. As if sensing the concern that is building as we watch, he is quick to reassure his audience: 'Now trust me, these were all *bad* guys.' (Of course, we don't trust him one tiny bit.) Our concern only increases as he tells us that 'they can evade ... pretty much any countermeasure. They *cannot* be stopped.' Another video rolls on the big screen, this one depicting a huge cargo aircraft that excretes thousands of these tiny drones, while we are informed that '[a] 25 million dollar budget now buys this – enough to kill half a city. The bad half.' (Just the bad half – yeah, riiiight.) 'Nuclear is obsolete', we are told. This new weapon offers the potential to 'take out your entire enemy, virtually risk-free'. What could possibly go wrong?

At that point the film cuts across to a fictional news feed that's designed to help us see the dirty reality behind the advocacy and smooth assurances presented by the Steve Jobs of Death. The weapon has fallen into the wrong hands. An attack on the US Capitol Building has killed eleven senators – all from 'just one side of the aisle'. TV news reports that 'the intelligence community has no idea who perpetrated the attack, nor whether it was a state, group, or even a single individual'. We witness the horror of a mother's Voice over the Internet Protocol [VOIP] call to her student-activist son that ends with his clinical killing by one of the micro drones, as swarms of them hunt down and murder thousands of university students at twelve universities across the world. The TV talking heads inform us that investigators are suggesting that the students may have been targeted because they shared a video on social media ostensibly 'exposing corruption at the highest level'. Then, suddenly, we're back on stage with Mr Death-Jobs, who tells us: 'Dumb weapons drop where you point. Smart weapons consume data. When you can find your enemy using data, even by a hashtag, you can target an evil ideology right where it starts.' He points to his temple as he speaks, so that we are left in no doubt as to just where that starting point is.

It's all very chilling, and it taps into some of our deepest fears and emotions. Weapons like tiny bugs that attach to your face just before exploding – creepy. Shadowy killers (states? terrorists? hyper-empowered individuals?) striking at will against helpless civilians for reasons we don't fully understand – frightening. People targeted on the basis of data gathered from social media – terrifying.

Slaughterbots was released to coincide with, and influence, the first of the 2017 Geneva meetings of the delegates working under the auspices of the United Nations' Convention on Conventional Weapons (CCW) to decide, on behalf of the international community, what (if anything) should be done about the emergence of lethal autonomous weapons systems (LAWS).[1] The year 2017 was the first year of formal meetings of the Group of Governmental Experts (GGE) on LAWS, though it followed on the heels of three years of informal meetings of experts tied to this process. At the time of writing, this international process continues. In addition to the state delegates to these meetings, a range of civil society groups are also represented, most notably the coalition of non-governmental organizations (NGOs) known as the Campaign to Stop Killer Robots. Originally launched in April 2013 on the steps of Britain's Parliament as

[1]   The formal name of the group is the Group of Governmental Experts on Emerging Technologies in the Area of Lethal Autonomous Weapons Systems (GGE LAWS) of the High Contracting Parties to the Convention on Prohibitions of Restrictions on the Use of Certain Conventional Weapons Which May Be Deemed to Be Excessively Injurious or to Have Indiscriminate Effects (CCW).

the Campaign to Ban Killer Robots, it was 'the Campaign' (as it is commonly known) that hosted the viewing of *Slaughterbots* at the 2017 GGE meeting in Geneva.

Slaughterbots certainly provided a significant boost to the Campaign's efforts to secure a ban on lethal autonomous weapons (or, failing a ban, to otherwise 'stop' these weapons). Unfortunately, the emotive reaction generated by the film is in large part the result of factors that are entirely irrelevant to the issue at hand: the question of *autonomous* weapons.

Remember what Russell identified as the key issue? '*Allowing machines to choose to kill humans*'. If you have time, watch the film again, and ask yourself this question throughout: what difference would it make to the scary scenarios in the film if, instead of the drones selecting and engaging their targets autonomously, a human being seated in front of a computer somewhere was watching through the drone's cameras and making the final call on who should or should not be killed? I don't mean just pressing the 'kill' button every time a red indicator flashes up on his or her screen – let's assume he or she takes the time to (say) check a photo and make sure that the person being killed is definitely on the kill list. To use a key term at the centre of the debate (which I will examine in depth in chapter 2), in this mental 'edit' of the film, a person is maintaining 'meaningful human control'.

In this alternative, imagined version, AI would still be vitally important in that it would allow the tiny quadcopters to fly, enable them to navigate through the corridors of Congress or Edinburgh University, and so on. But there are no serious suggestions that we should try to ban the use of AI in military autopilot and navigational systems, or even that we should ban military platforms that employ AI in order to carry out no-human-in-the-loop evasive measures to protect themselves. So that's not relevant to the key question at hand.

What about the nefarious uses to which these tiny drones are put in the film? It is, without question, deeply morally problematic, abhorrent even, that students should be killed because they shared or 'liked' a video online; but the fact that the targeting data were sourced from social media is an issue entirely independent of whether the final decision to kill this student or that was made by an algorithm or by a human being. Also irrelevant is the fact that autonomous weapons could in principle be used to carry out unattributed attacks: the same is true of a slew of both sophisticated and crude military capabilities, from cyberweapons to improvised explosive devices (IEDs), and even to antiquated bolt-action rifles. In short, a ban on autonomous weapons – even if adhered to – would make essentially no material difference to the frightening scenarios depicted in *Slaughterbots*.

There are real and important questions that need to be asked and answered about LAWS. But in order to make genuine progress we will need to disentangle those questions from the red herrings thrown up by *Slaughterbots* and, indeed, by many contributors to the debate. This book seeks to take steps in that direction by trying to give a clear answer to the question raised by the Campaign at its formation: should we *ban* these 'killer robots'? As campaigners rightly point out, this is a choice we have made before, in the case of other kinds of weapons systems: the international community has successfully negotiated treaties and agreements that have resulted in bans on military capabilities, including bans on chemical and biological weapons, antipersonnel landmines, and even blinding lasers. There's much that could be said about the process of securing such a ban, and what avenues might be available for doing so and to what effect, but that is not the question in focus here. Rather, this book is about whether or not we *should* ban LAWS.

To give you the bottom line up front, my answer to this question is in the negative. I hope to show here that the central considerations that have been raised in support of the view that we should ban (or in some other, undefined sense, 'stop') these systems are not, when put under scrutiny, ultimately convincing. This does not mean I think there should be no controls or constraints on the development and employment of LAWS; there certainly should be. Indeed, I have had the privilege of working alongside a group of international experts to try to outline a first attempt at a set of guiding principles for the international community now titled 'Guiding Principles for the Development and Use of LAWS'. But that is not the focus of this book. Instead, my argument here is focused on showing that we do not in fact have compelling reasons to *ban* 'killer robots'.

A Definition

Before proceeding, I do, of course, have to clarify what this phenomenon is that is the focus of our investigation. While 'killer robots' is much racier than 'lethal autonomous weapons', we are on firmer ground with the latter terminology; so, going forward, that is what I will generally use. So then, what exactly *is* a lethal autonomous weapon? There is, as yet, no universally accepted definition, and some parties to the debate have been accused (perhaps with some justification) of playing definitional games. There is, however, growing acceptance of the definition put forward by the International Committee of the Red Cross and Red Crescent (ICRC), according to which an autonomous weapon is

> [a]ny weapon system with autonomy in its critical functions. That is, a weapon system which can select (i.e. search for or detect, identify, track, select) and attack (i.e. use force against, neutralize, damage or destroy) targets without human intervention. (ICRC 2016, pp. 11–12, n. 2)

Despite being widely accepted, this definition is not without shortcomings. In particular, some of the terminology is, arguably, loaded. 'Select' carries an implication of deliberate cognitive activity, which may not be an appropriate description of how many autonomous weapons do or will function; 'discern' or 'identify' would be a more neutral alternative. Likewise, 'attack' is a loaded term in this context, given the importance of the question of the point at which human agency is relevant;

'engage' would, again, be a more neutral alternative. Nonetheless, for the purposes of this volume, I will take it that the ICRC definition is a sufficiently accurate description of the phenomenon under consideration to enable us to weigh up whether or not a ban is necessary.

I

Of War Dogs, Bat Bombs, Mercenaries and Killer Robots

'Shall I compare thee to a summer's day?' muses William Shakespeare as he reflects on the qualities of his beloved in the opening line of Sonnet 18. Plato, seeking to understand the nature of reality itself and our place in it, creates the famous allegory of a group of people chained in a fire-lit cave and watching shadows on the wall. These examples illustrate that, when we are wrestling with something that is challenging to express or comprehend, it is natural for us to reach for *analogies*. We look to other things that are relevantly similar, in the hope that they will help us to grasp the thing we are trying to understand. That can be very useful and we can learn a lot that way, but only if the analogy is well chosen (Shakespeare wouldn't have done particularly well if he'd decided to compare his beloved to a bit of pocket lint!).

While they have important antecedents, the lethal autonomous weapons systems (LAWS) that are on the near horizon (or, in some cases, already in production) are a new and challenging phenomenon, and so we naturally find ourselves looking for analogies that may help us to understand how to respond to them. Unfortunately, we often reach for unhelpful and unedifying analogies. Most common are analogies drawn from science fiction, whether it be the Schwarzenegger-shaped Terminator or the creepily measured tones of HAL 9000 from the classic movie *2001: A Space Odyssey*. The year 2001 was a long time ago, but we are still nowhere near having AI reach the level of general AI that could enable 'the machines' to turn against their human masters. The issue at hand is weapons that are *autonomous* – many of which are likely to be driven by relatively pedestrian algorithms – rather than weapons that have achieved a level of intelligence that matches or surpasses that of human beings (what is usually referred to as 'general AI'). There are certainly good reasons to be very cautious about developing weapons that incorporate general AI, but it's important to see that the questions to be asked are different from those we need to answer about autonomy in general. For one thing, if a system is that intelligent, then

13

we will have reached the point at which we need to decide whether the AI is capable of being held ethically and legally responsible for its actions. By contrast, as we will see, one of the main concerns about merely autonomous weapons is precisely that it is widely agreed that they *cannot* be held accountable, which opponents argue may leave an accountability gap.

So, if we are not to look to sci-fi for analogies that may help us to come to grips with the ethical issues associated with LAWS, what other options are available? A mostly overlooked but far more useful comparison is with *animals*.

The Dogs (and Horses, and Dolphins, and Pigeons, and Bats) of War

Animals have long been 'weaponized' (to use a term currently in vogue). The horses ridden by armoured knights in the Middle Ages were not mere transport. They were instead an integral part of the weapons system – they were taught to bite and kick, and the enemy was as likely to be trampled by the knight's horse as to taste the steel of his sword. There have been claims that US Navy dolphins 'have been trained in attack-and-kill missions since the Cold War' (Townsend 2005), though this has been strongly denied by official sources. Even more bizarrely, during the Second World War the noted behaviourist B. F. Skinner led an effort to develop a pigeon-controlled guided bomb, a precursor to today's guided anti-ship missiles. Using operant conditioning techniques, a pigeon housed within the weapon (which was essentially a steerable glide bomb) was trained to recognize an image of an enemy ship projected onto a small screen by lenses in the warhead. Should the image shift from the centre of the screen, the pigeon was trained to peck at the controls, which would adjust the bomb's steering mechanism, thereby putting it back on target. Despite what Skinner reports to have been a project of considerable promise, Project Pigeon (or Project ORCON – from 'organic control', as it became known after the war) was cancelled, largely as a result of improvements in electronic means of missile control (Skinner 1960).

The strangeness of Project Pigeon is matched or even exceeded by another Second World War initiative: Project X-Ray. Conceived by Lytle S. Adams, a dental surgeon and an acquaintance of First Lady Eleanor Roosevelt, this was an effort to weaponize *bats*. The plan was to attach small incendiary devices to Mexican free-tailed bats and airdrop them over Japanese cities. It was intended that, on release from their bomb-shaped delivery system, the bats would disperse and roost in eaves and attics, among the traditional wood-and-paper Japanese buildings. Once ignited by a small timer, the napalm-based incendiary would then start a fire that was expected to spread rapidly. The project was cancelled as efforts to develop the atomic bomb gained priority, but not before one accidental release of some 'armed' bats resulted in a fire at a US base that burned both a hangar and a general's car (Madrigal 2011).

The animals most commonly used as weapons, though, are probably dogs. An early example comes from the mid-seventh century BC, when the basic tactical unit of mounted forces from the Greek polis of Magnesia on the Maeander (present-day Ortaklar in Turkey) consisted of a horseman, a spear bearer and a war dog. It was recorded that the Magnesians' approach during their war against the Ephesians was to first release the dogs, who would break up the enemy ranks, then follow that up with a rain of spears, and finally complete the attack with a cavalry charge (Foster 1941, 115). Today, of course, dogs continue to play important military roles. They are trained and used as sentries and trackers, to detect mines and IEDs, and for crowd control. For the purposes of this book, though, it is the 'combat assault dogs' that accompany and support special operations forces that are of the greatest relevance.

These dogs are usually equipped with body-mounted video cameras and are trained to enter buildings and seek out the enemy. This enables the dog handler to reconnoitre enemy-held positions without in the process putting soldiers' lives at risk. New technologies are also being developed to enhance the human–dog team. For example, in October 2020 the US military announced that it was working with Command Sight Inc. to develop augmented reality glasses for military dogs. According to the press release, '[t]he augmented reality goggles are specially designed to fit each dog with a visual indicator that allows the dog to be directed to a specific spot and react to the visual cue in the goggles. The handler can see everything the dog sees to provide it commands through the glasses' (US Army 2020).

In addition to serving as a means of reconnaissance, combat assault dogs are also trained to attack anyone they discover who is armed (Norton-Taylor 2010). The dog itself is not usually responsible for killing the enemy combatant, instead it works to enable the soldiers it accompanies to employ lethal force; we might think of the dog as part of a lethal combat system. But at least one unconfirmed recent report indicates that it may not always be the case that the enemy is not directly killed by the combat assault dog. According to a newspaper report, in 2018 a British combat assault dog was part of a UK SAS patrol in northern Syria, when the patrol was ambushed. A source quoted in the report gave the following account:

> The handler removed the dog's muzzle and directed him into a building from where they were coming under fire. They could hear screaming and shouting before the firing from the house stopped. When the team entered the building they saw the dog standing over a dead gunman. . . . His throat had been torn out and he had bled to death . . . There was also a lump of human flesh in one corner and a series of blood trails leading out of the back of the building. The dog was virtually uninjured. The SAS was able to consolidate their defensive position and eventually break away from the battle without taking any casualties. (Martin 2018)

Are there any ethical issues of concern relating to the employment of dogs as weapons of war? I know of no published objections in this regard, beyond concerns for the safety and well-being of the dogs themselves,[2] which – given that the well-being of autonomous weapons is not an issue of interest here[3] – is not the sort of objection of relevance to this book. That, of course, is not to say that there are no ethical issues that might be raised here. I shall return to this question in what follows, in drawing a comparison between dogs, contracted combatants and autonomous weapons. First, though, I turn to consider what seems to me to be another useful analogy for LAWS, namely mercenaries or contracted combatants.

The 'Dogs of War'

In *Just Warriors, Inc: The Ethics of Privatized Force* (Baker 2011), I set out to explore the ethical objections to the employment of private military and security contractors in contemporary conflict zones. Are they mercenaries, and, if so, what is it

---

[2] For example, in an article on the UK SAS use of dogs in Afghanistan, the animal rights organization People for the Ethical Treatment of Animals (PETA) is quoted as saying that 'dogs are not tools or "innovations" and are not ours to use and toss away like empty ammunition shells' (Norton-Taylor 2010).

[3] But this is one of the issues we would have to take into consideration if we were talking about weapons incorporating general AI.

about mercenarism that is ethically objectionable? Certainly, the term 'mercenary' has predominantly pejorative connotations, which is why I chose to employ the neutral phrase 'contracted combatants' in my exploration, so as not to prejudge its outcome. Other common pejoratives for contracted combatants are 'whores of war' and 'dogs of war'. While 'whores of war' provides a fairly obvious clue to one of the normative objections to contracted combatants (to be discussed later), I did not address the pejorative 'dogs of war' in the book simply because I was unable at the time to identify any meaningful ethical problem associated with it. Perhaps, however, the analogy is a better fit than I then realized, as will become clear in the next pages. In what follows I outline the main arguments that emerged from my exploration in *Just Warriors, Inc.*

Perhaps the earliest thinker to explicitly address the issue of what makes contracted combatants ethically problematic is Niccolò Machiavelli, in *The Prince*. Two papers addressing the ethics of contracted combatants, one written by Anthony Coady (1992) and another by Tony Lynch and Adrian Walsh (2000), both take Machiavelli's comments as their starting point. According to these authors, Machiavelli's objections to mercenaries were effectively threefold:

1. Mercenaries are not sufficiently bloodthirsty.
2. Mercenaries cannot be trusted because of the temptations of political power.
3. There exists some motive or motives appropriate for engaging in war that mercenaries necessarily lack, or else mercenaries are motivated by some factor that is inappropriate for engaging in war.

The first of these points need not detain us long, for it is quite clear that, even if the empirically question-able claim that mercenaries lack the killing instinct necessary for war were true, this can hardly be considered a *moral* failing. But perhaps the point is instead one about effectiveness, the claim being that the soldier for hire cannot be relied upon to do what is necessary in battle when the crunch comes. But, even if this claim is true, it is evident that it cannot be the moral failing we are looking for either. For, while we might cast moral aspersions on such a mercenary, those aspersions would be in the family of such terms as 'feeble', 'pathetic' or 'hopeless'. But these are clearly not the *moral* failings we are looking for in trying to discover just what is wrong with being a mercenary. Indeed, the flip side of this objection seems to have more bite – namely the concern that mercenaries may be overly driven by 'killer instinct', that they might take undue pleasure in the business of causing death. This foreshadows the motivation objection discussed later.

Machiavelli's second point is even more easily dealt with. For it is quite clear that the temptation to grab power over a nation by force is at least as strong for national military forces as it is for mercenaries. It could even be argued that mercenaries are more reliable in this respect. For example, a comprehensive analysis of coup trends in Africa between 1956 and 2001 addressed 80 successful coups, 108 unsuccessful coup attempts and 139 reported coup plots; out of these, only four coup plots involved mercenaries – and all four were led by the same man, the Frenchman Bob Denard (McGowan 2003).

Machiavelli's third point is, of course, the most widespread objection to mercenarism: the concern over *motivation*. The most common version of this objection claims that there is something wrong with fighting for money; this is the basis for the pejorative description of mercenaries as 'whores of war'. As Lynch and Walsh point out, however, the objection cannot simply be that the desire for money is a morally questionable motivation for action. For, while a case could perhaps be made for this view, it would apply to such a wide range of human activities that it offers little help in discerning what singles out mercenarism as especially problematic.

Perhaps, then, the problem is being motivated by money above all else. Lynch and Walsh helpfully suggest that we label such a person a 'lucrepath'. By this thinking, 'those criticising mercenaries for taking blood money are then accusing them of being lucrepaths ... it is not that they do things for money but that money is the *sole* or the *dominant* consideration in their practical deliberations' (Lynch and Walsh 2000, 136).

A variant of the improper motivation argument is that mercenaries might be motivated by blood lust. But, of course, it is empirically doubtful that this applies to all contracted combatants, and there is also every likelihood that those motivated by blood lust will be just as likely to seek to satisfy that lust through service in regular military forces.

Perhaps, then, the question of appropriate motives is not that mercenaries are united by having a particular, morally reprehensible motive, but rather that they *lack* a particular motive that is necessary for good moral standing when it comes to fighting and killing. What might such a motive be? Most commentators identify two main candidates, namely 'just cause' and 'right intention', as defined by just war theory. As Lynch and Walsh (2000, 138) put it, '[e]x *hypothesi*, killing in warfare is justifiable only when the soldier in question is motivated amongst

23

other things by a just cause. Justifiable killing motives must not only be non-lucrepathic, but also, following Aquinas, must include just cause and right intention'. The argument, then, is that, whatever it is that actually motivates contracted combatants, it is not the desire to satisfy the just cause that is their motivation, and therefore they do not fight with right intention. While I did not consider this when I wrote *Just Warriors, Inc.*, it is worth noting here that this objection cuts in two directions. Directed against the otherwise motivated contracted combatant, it paints him or her as morally lacking, on the grounds that the good combatant ought to be motivated in this way. The objection also points to implications for those on the receiving end of the lethal actions carried out by the contracted combatant. Here the idea is that to fail to be motivated by the just cause is at the same time to show a lack of respect for one's opponents. Put in broadly Kantian terms, to fight with any motivation other than the desire to achieve the just cause is to use the enemy as a *mere means* to satisfy some other end – whether that be pecuniary advantage, blood lust, adventurism or whatever.[4] In

[4] In *Just Warriors, Inc.* I discussed a number of other motives (or lack thereof) that might be considered morally problematic. In the interest of brevity I have set those motives aside here.

other words, it violates the *dignity* of those on the receiving end.

Moving on from Machiavelli's list, we find that another frequent objection to the use of contracted combatants focuses on the question of *accountability*. One vector of this objection is the claim that the use of contracted combatants undermines democratic control over the use of force. There is a strong argument, for example, that the large-scale use of contractors in Iraq under the Bush administration was, at least in part, an attempt to circumvent congressional limitations on the number of troops which could be deployed into that theatre. Another regularly expressed concern is that the availability of contracted combatants offers a means whereby governments can avoid existing controls on their use of force by using private contractors to undertake 'black' operations.[5]

Another vector of the accountability objection relates to punishment. If convicted of offences under military law (such as the Uniform Code of Military Justice, which applies to US military personnel), members of a state's military face punishments ranging from dismissal from the military

---

[5] Blackwater, for example, was accused of carrying out assassinations and illegal renditions of detainees on behalf of the CIA (Steingart 2009).

to imprisonment and, in some extreme cases, to execution. It has been a source of significant concern among critics of the private military industry that private military companies and their employees are not subject to the same rigorous standards of justice as state military employees. Beyond this consequentialist concern there is, further, the deontological concern that justice will not be done for actions that would be punishable under law if these actions were carried out by uniformed military personnel.

The final primary concern regarding the outsourcing of armed forces by states is that private contractors undermine appropriate levels of *control*. This is not quite the same concern over trustworthiness that Machiavelli expressed, but it is similar. At the strategic level, the worry is that the outsourcing of traditional military functions into private hands could in principle undermine civil–military relations – ideally, the relationship of subservience between the military and their elected leaders (also known as democratic control of armed forces). The objection made by many opponents of military privatization is that it is inappropriate to delegate military tasks to non-governmental organizations. Peter W. Singer, for example, writes: 'When the government *delegates* out part of its role in national security through the recruitment and maintenance of armed forces, it is abdicating an essential responsibility'[6] (Singer 2003, 226, italics added). Contracted combatants are perceived by many as out-of-control 'cowboys'. Of particular relevance here is the worry that, if contracted combatants cannot be adequately controlled, they may well act in violation of important norms, including the principles of international humanitarian law.

To sum up, then, the main lines of objection that have been raised to the employment of contracted combatants are those of *motivation* (which includes the question of respecting human *dignity*), *control* and *accountability*, and *reliability* and *trustworthiness*. I have dealt with these objections to contracted combatants in some detail (see Baker 2011), and it is not my intention to repeat here in any depth the arguments contained in that book. What I hope to show, however, is that, just like the literal dogs of war, the metaphorical dogs of war provide us with a very helpful analogy for thinking through the ethical objections that have been raised against the employment of autonomous weapons systems.

---

[6] As this is not an objection with a clear parallel in the case of autonomous weapons (or combat assault dogs, for that matter), I will set it aside here. I address this issue in chapter 6 of *Just Warriors, Inc.*

The Robot Dogs of War

Paulo and two squad mates huddled together in the trenches, cowering while hell unfolded around them. Dozens of mechanical animals the size of large dogs had just raced through their position, rifle fire erupting from gun barrels mounted between their shoulder blades. The twisted metal remains of three machines lay in the dirt in front of their trenches, destroyed by the mines. The remaining machines had headed towards the main camp yipping like hyenas on the hunt. Two BMPs exploded in their wake. Paulo had seen one of the machines leap at his battalion commander and slam the officer in the chest with a massive, bone crunching thud. It spun away from the dying officer, pivoting several times to shoot at the [Russian advisors deployed with Paulo's unit]. Two of them fell dead, the third ran. It turned and followed the other machines deeper into the camp. Paulo heard several deep BOOMs outside the perimeter he recognized as mortars firing and moments later fountains of dirt leapt skyward near the closest heavy machine gun bunker. The bunker was struck and exploded. Further away a string of explosions traced over the trench line, killing several men. In the middle of it all he swore he heard a cloud of insects buzzing and looked up to see what looked like a small swarm of bird-sized creatures flying overhead. They ignored him and kept going. (Matson n.d.)

This rather terrifying scenario is an extract from 'Demons in the Long Grass', a fictional account, by the writer Mike Matson, of a near-future battle involving imagined autonomous weapons systems. Handily for the purposes of this chapter, some of the autonomous weapons systems described are dog-like – the 'robot dogs of war'; and the author says that these were inspired by footage of Boston Dynamics' robot dog Spot (Matson 2018). The scariness of the scenario taps into a range of deep-seated human fears, but the fact that a weapon system is frightening is not in itself a reason for objecting to it (though it seems likely that this is what lies behind many of the more vociferous calls for a ban on LAWS). Thankfully, the philosophers Filippo Santoni de Sio and Jeroen van den Hoven have put forward a clear and unemotional summary of the primary ethical objections to autonomous weapons, and I find no reason to dispute their account. They point out that the ethical objections that have been raised in the debate over LAWS fall into three main areas:

(a) [A]s a matter of fact, robots of the near future will not be capable of making the sophisticated practical and moral distinctions required by the laws of armed conflict . . .: distinction between combatants and non-combatants, proportionality in the use of force, and military necessity of violent action. . . .

(b) As a matter of principle, it is morally wrong to let a machine be in control of the life and death of a human being, no matter how technologically advanced the machine is . . . According to this position . . . these applications are *mala in se* [evils in their own right] . . .

(c) In the case of war crimes or fatal accidents, the presence of an autonomous weapon system in the operation may make it more difficult, or impossible altogether, to hold military personnel morally and legally responsible. (Santoni de Sio and van den Hoven 2018, 2)

A similar summary is provided by the ICRC (2018, 9): 'Ethical arguments against autonomous weapon systems can generally be divided into two forms: objections based on the limits of technology to function within legal constraints and ethical norms; and ethical objections that are independent of technological capability'. The latter set of objections includes the questions of whether the use of autonomous weapons might lead to 'a responsibility gap where humans cannot uphold their moral responsibility' and might undermine 'the human dignity of those combatants who are targeted, and of civilians who are put at risk of death and injury as a consequence of attacks on legitimate military targets', and discusses the possibility that 'further increasing human distancing – physically and psychologically – from the battlefield' could increase 'existing asymmetries' and make 'the use of violence easier or less controlled'.

It is clear that the two summaries raise essentially the same objections. It is also clear that these objections correspond closely to the objections to contracted contractors discussed so far. That is, both contracted combatants and autonomous weapons face opposition on the grounds that they are morally problematic on account of deficits in trustworthiness or reliability, challenges in establishing appropriate levels of control and associated concerns over accountability, and appropriateness of motivation (which includes the question of respecting human dignity). And, while there are no published objections to the employment of weaponized animals that I am aware of, it doesn't take much imagination to see that, were such objections to be raised, they would more than likely fall into the same categories.

In the remainder of this book, I will therefore employ this framework of questions as the means of exploring the idea that LAWS should be banned under international law. I begin, in the next chapter, by examining an objection to LAWS that is based on claims that these systems cannot be trusted to operate reliably within the bounds of the ethical and legal constraints that apply to the use of force in armed conflict. Chapter 3 focuses on whether deficiencies of control and inadequate accountability should lead us to pursue a ban on these systems. Chapter 4 addresses what many argue is the weightiest objection to the development and employment of LAWS. Here the objection is that their use constitutes ceding to a machine the right to choose to kill human beings and thereby undermines the dignity of those whose lives are thus taken. As I have already indicated, my position is that, while all of these are important considerations, none of them (and no combination of them) is sufficiently weighty to warrant instituting a ban on LAWS. Nonetheless I recognize that deeply held and irreconcilable moral intuitions may prevent us from reaching consensus on this issue. I therefore focus, in the final chapter, on outlining an appropriate methodology for policymakers who represent liberal states to employ as they seek to come to a position on whether to ban 'killer robots'.

2

Trust, Trustworthiness and Reliability

It no longer surprises us that computers can beat us at strategy games. The idea that a supercomputer can beat the best human chess players is now commonplace. But when, in the spring of 2016, Google's AI known as AlphaGo played against South Korea's Lee Se-dol in the ancient Japanese game of Go (weiqi or wei-ch'i in Chinese), the world sat up and took notice. Go is widely acknowledged as one of the most complex games in existence: there are more possible configurations in the game than atoms in the known universe. Lee Se-dol is among the very best – in the game's own language, a 9-dan professional. Over a series of five games, AlphaGo won four games to Lee's one. It was the first time a 9-dan Go professional had ever been beaten by a computer. A year later an even more powerful version of AlphaGo, dubbed 'Master', comprehensively defeated the world's number one Go player, Ke Jie, in a series of three games.

This groundbreaking achievement by an AI was very much noted in military circles. The People's Liberation Army (PLA) in China responded with particular enthusiasm and urgently arranged a series of high-level seminars and symposia on the topic. According to Elsa Kania, an expert on Chinese defence innovation, in Chinese military circles the achievement of AlphaGo and its successors is considered to be 'a turning point that demonstrated the potential of AI to engage in complex analyses and strategizing comparable to that required to wage war – not only equalling human cognitive capabilities but even contributing a distinctive advantage that may surpass the human mind' (Kania 2017, 15).

Although the only human ever to win a game against AlphaGo (out of seventy-eight games played involving a human opponent), Lee Se-dol retired from the game not long afterwards, noting in his statement to the press: 'Even if I become the number one, there is an entity that cannot be defeated' (quoted in Vincent 2019). He was not exaggerating: though Lee was able to beat AlphaGo in one game, the most recent variant of AlphaGo, AlphaGo Zero, defeated the original version of AlphaGo one hundred times without loss during its 'training'. Many observers were unsettled by the now famous move 37 made by AlphaGo in game 2 against Lee. That move was initially thought to be a mistake but turned out to be the winning move. Why was it so unsettling? Because there is wide agreement that *it was a move that no human player would ever have made.*

The spectre of AlphaGo, and particularly of move 37, looms large in the debate over lethal autonomous weapons systems (LAWS). How, critics ask, can we trust an algorithm-controlled weapons system, when it has the potential to do things that we cannot foresee and that a human would not have done? More broadly, can we ever trust a weapons system that can select and attack targets without human intervention?

The first question we must ask here is this: just what is it that we want from trust in this context? Michael Lewis, Katia Sycara and Phillip Walker have reviewed the relevant scholarly literature on trust and provided this summary:

> it is generally agreed that trust is best conceptualized as a *multidimensional psychological attitude* involving beliefs and expectations about the trustee's trustworthiness derived from experience and interactions with the trustee in situations of uncertainty and

risk. Trust has also been said to have both *cognitive and affective features*. In the interpersonal literature, trust is also seen as involving affective processes, since trust development requires seeing others as personally motivated by care and concern to protect the trustor's interests. In the automation literature, cognitive (rather than affective) processes may play a dominant role in the determination of trustworthiness, i.e. the extent to which automation is expected to do the task that it was designed to do. In the trust in automation literature it has been argued that trust is best conceptualized as an attitude, and a relatively well accepted definition of trust is: '... an attitude which includes the belief that the collaborator will perform as expected, and can, within the limits of the designer's intentions, be relied on to achieve the designer's goals.' (Lewis et al. 2018, 137)

One key point we can take away from this is that there is an important difference between trust and trustworthiness. Trust is about our attitude to a certain thing or person, whereas trustworthiness is about the nature of that thing or person. So, something or someone may be trust*worthy*, but – for various reasons to do with human psychology – may still not be trust*ed*. Consider, for example, the many strangers you pass in the street every day. It's likely that a number of them are trustworthy individuals (honest, caring, reliable, etc.), but you are nonetheless unlikely to trust a random stranger with your wallet or child.

For the purposes of this book, what matters is the trustworthiness (or lack thereof) of LAWS, not the broader question of trust. That's not to say that trust is not important in this context. If we decide that developing and employing LAWS is ethically acceptable, we will still need to understand and address important issues that emerge from the human psychology of trust. For example, we will need to address the issue of overtrusting, as it is well documented that humans are susceptible to what is known as 'algorithm bias' – the propensity to trust an algorithm to deliver outcomes beyond what it was designed to achieve.[7] But these kinds of issues must be separated from the question of whether or not the LAWS themselves are trustworthy.

What is it, exactly, that opponents to LAWS believe we cannot trust LAWS to do? As we saw from Santoni de Sio and van den Hoven's (2018, 2) summary of the objections raised against LAWS,

[7] It is important not to confuse 'algorithm bias' (the tendency for humans to overtrust the deliverances of algorithms) with 'algorithmic bias', which is what occurs when bias (e.g. gender or racial bias) is (usually unintentionally) baked into an algorithm.

one main vector is the concern that 'robots of the near future will not be capable of making the sophisticated practical and moral distinctions required by the laws of armed conflict . . .: distinction between combatants and non-combatants, proportionality in the use of force, and military necessity of violent action'.

Is this true? Are LAWS untrustworthy because they cannot be relied upon to operate in accordance with the principles of distinction, proportionality and necessity? Human Rights Watch (HRW) is one organization that holds precisely this view. In a 2016 memorandum addressed to the delegates of the Convention on Conventional Weapons (CCW), HRW contended:

> Determining whether an individual is a legitimate target often depends on the capacity to detect and interpret subtle cues, such as tone of voice and body language. Humans usually understand such nuances because they can identify with other human beings and thus better gauge their intentions. Assessing proportionality entails a case-by-case analysis, traditionally based on a reasonable commander standard. Such an analysis requires 'distinctively human judgement' and the application of reason, which takes into account both moral and legal considerations. (Human Rights Watch 2016)

The fairly obvious problem here is that very few humans involved in selecting and engaging enemy targets on today's battlefields are even remotely in a position to interpret cues such as tone of voice and body language. Yes, this might *sometimes* apply to (say) an infantry soldier manning a checkpoint during a counterinsurgency campaign. But the sniper providing overwatch will not be able to hear the target's tone of voice, and the Reaper pilot observing through the cameras located under his remotely piloted aircraft's fuselage will have even less ability to interpret such cues. And what of the fast jet pilot delivering a 500-pound bomb onto a building that intelligence has identified as an insurgent command post? Her ability to pick up on tone of voice and body language is nil. So, does this mean that, in carrying out her mission, the pilot fails to meet the necessary epistemic standard required to ensure that appropriate constraints are adhered to? Have considerations of discrimination, necessity and proportionality simply been discarded? Of course not – because the operational context is different. If we were to apply HRW's epistemic standard across all military uses of force, we would essentially rule out the use of almost all standoff weapons, not just LAWS!

Part of the problem here, it seems to me, is that the armed conflicts of the last decade and more have primarily been low-intensity counterinsurgency conflicts, and many commentators have unthinkingly taken the constraints that apply in such conflicts to be the norm for all forms of war. That, of course, is not at all true; the appropriate application of the legal and ethical principles that regulate war looks significantly different in the context of high-intensity wars between states that are peer adversaries. As Valerie Morkevičius rightly points out, '[j]ust war thinking must pay careful attention to new developments in tactics, technologies and organizational strategies' (to include, of course, the emergence of LAWs), but in so doing it must avoid two pitfalls: 'We must not allow our understanding of just war to be dependent on a particular version of what war looks like'; and 'we must also not allow ourselves to be so historically focused or so theoretically minded as to fail to appreciate the very real challenges new developments in war pose to our traditional principles. One way to remain engaged is to pay close attention to the dilemmas of warfare as understood by practitioners' (Morkevičius 2018, 226).

The ICRC expresses a similar concern to that of HRW, placing particular emphasis on the distinction between what it calls 'specific' and 'generalized' targeting:

> The key difference between a human or remote-controlled weapon and an autonomous weapon system is that the former involves a human choosing a specific target – or group of targets – to be attacked, connecting their moral (and legal) responsibility to the specific consequences of their actions. In contrast, an autonomous weapon system self-initiates an attack: it is given a technical description, or a 'signature', of a target, and a spatial and temporal area of autonomous operation. This description might be general ('an armoured vehicle') or even quite specific ('a certain type of armoured vehicle'), but the key issue is that the commander or operator activating the weapon is not giving instructions on a specific target to be attacked ('specific armoured vehicle') at a specific place ('at the corner of that street') and at a specific point in time ('now'). Rather, when activating the autonomous weapon system, by definition, the user will not know exactly which target will be attacked ('armoured vehicles fitting this technical signature'), in which place (within x square kilometres) or at which point in time (during the next x minutes/hours). Thus, it can be argued, this more generalized nature of the targeting decision means the user is not applying their intent to each specific attack. (ICRC 2018)

This description clearly fits well with something like the Harop loitering munition, which is manufactured by Israel Aerospace Industries. When employed in autonomous mode (it can also be operated with a human in the loop), the Harop is designed to loiter over the designated target area, using its inbuilt sensors to detect radio emissions associated with air defence systems. Once one is detected, the Harop homes in on the signal and detonates its explosive warhead. Clearly this is the sort of generalized targeting that the ICRC is concerned about: the commander or operator of the system is not instructing the Harop to engage a particular radar system at a particular location and at a specific time. But so what? The fact is that the level of specificity that is being demanded in the ICRC statement above is frequently not met when traditional standoff weapons systems are used. When a weapons systems officer on an anti-submarine warfare (ASW) helicopter launches a Mark 46 acoustic homing torpedo in response to a fleeting sonar contact, she does not direct that torpedo to engage a particular submarine at a particular time and in a particular location. Rather, her intent is that the weapons should engage any submarine within range of the system and at some time during the system's endurance, when and if the acoustic homing system of the torpedo detects one. If there is more than one enemy submarine in the vicinity and the torpedo strikes one that was not the original sonar contact, so be it! The Mark 46 torpedo is essentially the underwater version of an autonomous loitering munition – yet no one has ever suggested that, when a Mark 46 torpedo destroys a subsurface target, the user is not applying her intent to the attack (the Mark 46 has been in service since the early 1960s).

Consider also an artillery battery conducting counterbattery fire, directed by a radar system that can track and plot incoming enemy artillery shells. Such a counterbarrage will seek to hit not only the artillery pieces the enemy is using to fire the incoming artillery shells, but also any enemy personnel, vehicles and equipment in the unit that operates those artillery pieces, even though the commander of the battery in question may well not know the specifics of those additional targets. Although the target is thus somewhat 'generalized' (to use the ICRC term) and those conducting the counterbattery fire do not know precisely what enemy personnel they will be hitting in the near vicinity of the enemy's artillery pieces, killing or disabling all enemy personnel within that geographical space is clearly within the scope of their intent. The addition of LAWS to the battlefield seems, if anything, to enable greater specificity. Rather than being limited to saturating a specific geographical area with high explosive munitions, employing a well-designed LAWS potentially allows for the addition of further parameters, which give greater opportunities for specificity in the application of the targeteer's intent.

The concern underlying the ICRC's objection is not really about intent (which I will address separately, alongside 'motive', in chapter 4), but rather, as in the HRW objection considered earlier, about the appropriate epistemic conditions for killing in war. This is a legitimate concern, but one that must be weighed appropriately: we cannot reasonably apply epistemic standards that do not apply to other types of weapons systems that are already in use and accepted as legally and ethically uncontroversial. Nor must we overstate the level of epistemic advantage available to individual human combatants on the ground. Their situational awareness will be impacted by factors that won't impact a LAWS in like circumstances – factors such as fear, adrenaline or fatigue.

Of course, there are those who would be prepared to bite the bullet and argue that, if the epistemic conditions for ethical trustworthiness in the application of force that LAWS are being held up against are not met by other weapons systems, then so much the worse for those systems. They should not be used, regardless of the impact that this would have on the capacity to wage war. But this is to misunderstand the nature of the just war tradition. If we are to successfully position the idea of the just war between the untenable extremes of pacifism and 'all's fair in love and war' realism, we must recognize (as Morkevičius argues) that the just war tradition has to be positioned closer to realism than to pacifism. If we accept that wars must sometimes be fought – and, indeed, that this can be the morally appropriate thing to do – then we cannot accept constraints on the use of force in war that in effect amount to a form of pacifism, because they make the effective conduct of any actual wars impossible to justify. As Tony Coates (1997, 100) rightly puts it, the appropriate way to think about the ethics of war is not just a matter 'of bringing the principles to bear upon the facts, but of bringing the relevant facts to bear on the principles'.

So the epistemic conditions we set as requirements for the ethical trustworthiness of LAWS must be reasonable. If awareness of the human adversary's tone of voice or body language is not a requirement for a fast-jet pilot to be considered ethically sound in her targeting decisions, then it doesn't make sense to make this a sweeping test for LAWS. And if a degree of generalization in targeting is appropriate for artillery batteries and for homing torpedoes, then counting LAWS as ethically problematic because their employment means giving up 'specificity' is equally puzzling.

Of course, there are many situations on the battlefield where a fast jet delivering a 500-pound bomb or an artillery battery delivering a barrage of shells would be legally and ethically inappropriate as means to achieve a legitimate military end. Context matters, and the same applies to the use of LAWS.

In their study of trust in the context of automation, Lewis and his colleagues find that, '[i]n terms of environmental factors that influence trust in automation, risk seems most important. Research in trust in automation suggests that reliance on automation is modulated by the risk present in the decision to use the automation' (Lewis et al. 2018, 141). The intersection of risk and trustworthiness is reflected in the concept of 'boxed autonomy' – the idea that LAWS could be allowed to operate autonomously within an operational 'box' predefined by target parameters, a fixed time period and geospatial constraints. Some environments generate greater risk than others that the use of an autonomous weapons system will result in *ius in bello* violations. Combat in a crowded urban environment, for example, is ethically far riskier than, say, subsurface anti-submarine warfare. Because it is exceedingly unlikely that an autonomous weapons system will encounter non-combatants in the subsurface environment and because questions of necessity and proportionality seldom arise in anti-submarine warfare, the risk of ethical failure in this environment is low. So there are environments in which employing even a relatively unsophisticated autonomous weapon might be appropriate (the Mark 46 anti-submarine torpedo, is, arguably, just such a weapon), and there are environments in which using such a weapon would not be appropriate. This is of course true of all weapons systems. For example, there are environments where the use of highly destructive weapons – such as the infamous GBU-43/B Massive Ordnance Air Blast Bomb, known as the 'mother of all bombs' – would clearly be inappropriate. But using such a weapon against a massed enemy fleet at sea, for example, would be entirely acceptable. For LAWS, it will always be necessary to evaluate whether the *particular* system we are dealing with is capable of reliably operating within reasonably assessed levels of ethical and legal risk in a *particular* context and environment. It would be entirely appropriate, for example, to allow a sophisticated air-superiority unmanned combat air vehicle (UCAV) to operate autonomously and weapons-free in bounded airspace above a naval battle group on the open seas during an attack by an opposing naval force. On the other hand, allowing that same UCAV to operate autonomously and weapons-free in airspace where there is only a small possibility of enemy aircraft being present and where there is a high likelihood of civilian aircraft transiting the airspace box may not be appropriate – unless that system is extremely well proven in its ability to distinguish enemy military aircraft from civilian aircraft.

In addition to reliability and environment, an important related factor is predictability. Interestingly, Lewis and his colleagues point out that even an unreliable system, one that is known to suffer from system faults, can be trusted when those faults are predictable. 'Research has shown that when people have prior knowledge of faults, these faults do not necessarily diminish trust in the system. A plausible explanation is that knowing that the automation may fail reduces the uncertainty and consequent risk associated with use of the automation. In other words, predictability may be as (or more) important as reliability' (Lewis et al. 2018, 140). Here we return to the question raised by AlphaGo and move 37: can we trust an algorithm-driven weapons system if its behaviour is not predictable, just as AlphaGo showed itself to be unpredictable?

Before answering this question, it is worth reiterating that, if we go by the most widely accepted definition of LAWS – that they are weapons systems that can 'select . . . and attack . . . targets without human intervention' – then such systems need not be particularly sophisticated. The algorithm guiding a Harop loitering munition is orders of magnitude less sophisticated and capable than AlphaGo and its successors; and, importantly, it is not a self-learning system in the way AlphaGo is. There is thus no inherent reason why its behaviour should be unpredictable; barring any system faults, it will simply do what it has been programmed to do. It is therefore a mistake to suppose, as Kate Devitt (2018, 162) does, that it is an inherent feature of autonomous systems that they 'learn and adapt in their environments rendering their actions more indeterminate over time'.

Of course, this only narrows rather than resolves the question at hand. While it is not the case that all LAWS are by their nature unpredictable, those that are designed to 'learn and adapt' will almost certainly act, as AlphaGo did, in ways that are unexpected, or perhaps even (in the strict sense) *unpredictable*. But, while this may make it psychologically difficult for us to trust such a system, it does not necessarily make the system itself untrustworthy. Move 37 was unexpected, perhaps even unpredictable, but at no point did AlphaGo behave in an *untrustworthy* manner. It pursued, without exception, the goal it had been programmed to pursue – to win the game against its opponent – and remained 100 per cent compliant with the constraints it had been programmed to operate within – the rules of Go. Trustworthiness and unpredictability are therefore not mutually exclusive conditions. Indeed, the ability of AlphaGo to reliably achieve the task it was set – winning a game of Go against its opponent – turned out to depend, at least in part, on its ability to be unpredictable. Likewise, for some kinds of LAWS, the ability to act unpredictably within appropriately defined bounds will be precisely what accounts for their ability to defeat an enemy combatant or a system in combat. The ICRC's (2021) contention that '[u]npredictable autonomous weapon systems should be expressly ruled out, notably because of their indiscriminate effects', is clearly lacking in nuance.

Consider again the comparison we have been drawing between LAWS and weaponized dogs.

There are unquestionably environments in which it would be inappropriate to employ combat assault dogs, given the degree of control that is available to the handler (which will differ depending on such variables as the kind and extent of training, the character of the particular dog, etc.), and the same holds for autonomous weapons systems. Likewise, it goes without saying that there are ways in which autonomous weapons systems could be used that would make violations of the international humanitarian law likely. But these problems are contingent on specific contextual questions about environment and design; they do not amount to intrinsic objections to autonomous weapons systems.

What do we learn if we turn our attention to our other comparandum, the figurative 'dogs of war'? The question of whether contracted combatants can be trusted is often framed as a concern about the character of these 'mercenaries'. But, as I argue elsewhere, this is mainly to look in the wrong direction (Baker 2011). Peter Feaver (2003) points out in his book *Armed Servants* that the same problem afflicts much of the literature on civil–military relations, which tends to focus on 'soft' aspects of the relationship between the military and civilian leaders, particularly the presence or absence of military professionalism and subservience. But, as

Feaver shows, the issue is less about trustworthiness than it is about *control*. He shows that civilian principles in fact employ a wide range of control mechanisms in order to ensure – in the language of principal–agent theory – that the military is 'working' rather than 'shirking'.[8] In *Just Warriors, Inc.*, I draw on Feaver's agency theory to show that the same control measures do – or at least can – apply to contracted combatants.

While those specific measures do not pertain directly to autonomous weapons systems, the same broad point holds: focusing only on the systems themselves misses the broad range of mechanisms of control that are applied to the use of weapons systems in general and that are, or can be, applied to autonomous weapons. It is worth considering again the analogy with combat assault dogs. To focus entirely on the dogs' capacity for autonomous action, and therefore to conclude that their employment in war is intrinsically morally inappropriate, would be to ignore the range of control measures that military combat dog handlers ('commanders')

---

8   In principal–agent theory, 'shirking' has a technical meaning, which extends beyond that of 'goofing off' (i.e. the sense of 'shirk' in everyday usage). In this technical sense, for agents to be shirking, they must do anything but what the principal intends them to do. Agents can thus be working hard (in the normal understanding of the word) and still be shirking.

have available to them. If we can reasonably talk about the controlled use of military combat dogs, then perhaps we can take seriously the idea that LAWS are able to retain their capacity for autonomy while still being appropriately controlled. I explore this question in the next chapter.

3

Control and Accountability

The core contested notion in the debate over lethal autonomous weapons systems (LAWS) has, for some time, been the idea of meaningful human control. For example, a 2016 report authored by the UN special rapporteurs on extrajudicial, summary or arbitrary executions and on the rights to freedom of peaceful assembly and of association proposed that '[a]utonomous weapons systems that require no meaningful human control should be prohibited' (UN 2016, 15). Few would disagree with this. The difficulty, however, is that much of the discussion on meaningful human control is saturated with claims and assumptions that, on closer inspection, turn out to be problematic. What, precisely, does it mean for us to be in control of a weapons system? Is it possible to be in control of an *autonomous* weapon? Can anyone be held accountable, in other words bear responsibility for the outcome, if the employment of an autonomous weapon results in a war crime? We generally hold people responsible for events that are under their control (or for events over which they should have exercised control), but is this possible when it is LAWS that are doing the killing? Before considering these questions as they apply to LAWS, it is worth pausing to reflect on the two comparanda that have guided us thus far: contracted combatants (the figurative dogs of war) and weaponized animals (the actual dogs of war).

In my analysis of the ethical concerns over the employment of contracted combatants, concerns over control were pre-eminent. Contracted combatants fit uncomfortably within the framework of traditional accounts of civil–military relations (aka the democratic control of armed forces) such as the one put forward by Samuel Huntington. For Huntington, the key factors in appropriate civil–military relations are what we might call 'soft' factors, in particular the internalization, among military personnel, of a military ethic that 'exalts obedience as the highest virtue of military men' (Huntington 1957, 49). As mentioned at the end of the previous chapter, I draw instead on Peter Feaver's (2003) agency theory of civil–military relations, which derives from principal–agent theory and outlines how states actually employ a wide range of 'hard' compliance mechanisms to ensure that the military aligns with the interests and intentions of the elected civilian principals. Control is therefore possible, and it is consequently also possible to ensure accountability. While there are justifiable concerns about holding contracted combatants accountable for their actions, again, these concerns arise from contingent circumstances rather than from the intrinsic nature of the outsourcing of military force. As I argued earlier, there is in principle no reason why civilian principals cannot either put in place penal codes that apply specifically to private military companies and their employees, or else expand existing military law to cover private warriors. For example, in 2006 the US Congress extended the scope of the Uniform Code of Military Justice so as to ensure its applicability to private military contractors. While it remains to be seen whether endeavours such as these will withstand the inevitable legal challenges, they clearly indicate that there is in principle no reason why states cannot use penal codes to punish private military agents.

The situation with LAWS is a little different. In this case it *is* an intrinsic feature of these systems that raises the concern: the fact that the operator or commander of the system does not directly select and approve the particular target that is engaged. Some of those who object to LAWS therefore argue that, because the weapons system itself cannot be held accountable, the requirement of accountability cannot be satisfied, or cannot be satisfied in full. Here the situation is most closely analogous to that of the combat assault dog. Once released by her handler, the combat assault dog (particularly when she is out of sight of her handler, or her handler is otherwise occupied) selects and engages targets autonomously. The graphic 'dog rips out terrorist's throat' story recounted earlier is a case in point. Once inside the building that hosted the terrorists, the Special Air Service (SAS) dog selected and engaged her targets without further intervention from her handler. The question is, then, do we think that there is a problem with accountability in such cases?

While I know of no discussion of this topic in the context of combat assault dogs, in domestic law addressing dangerous dogs the answer is clear: the owner or the handler is held to be liable for any undue harm caused. Dogs that cause undue harm to humans are often 'destroyed' (killed) as a consequence; but there is no sense in which this is a punishment for the dog. Rather it is the relevant human who is held accountable, while the dog is killed as a matter of public safety. Of course, liability in such cases is not *strict* liability: we do not hold the owner or handler responsible for the harm caused *regardless* of the circumstances. If the situation that led to the dog's unduly harming someone were such that the owner or the handler could not have reasonably foreseen the situation arising, then the owner or the handler would not be held liable. Let us go back to our military combat dog example. What if the SAS dog had ripped the throat out of someone who was merely a passer-by, who happened to have picked up an AK-47 she found lying in the street, and who had then unknowingly sought shelter in the same building from which the terrorists were executing their ambush? That would be tragic, but it hardly seems that there is an accountability gap in this case. Given the right to use force in self-defence, as the SAS patrol did in this case, and given the inevitability of epistemic uncertainty amid the fog of war, some tragedies happen for which nobody is to blame.

We can take it, then, that, if control is possible, so is accountability. In what follows I will therefore focus on the question of whether it is possible to have an appropriate degree of control over LAWS. The concept of meaningful human control has become increasingly influential in the discussions in and around the meetings of the Group of Governmental Experts that addresses the issue of LAWS, and is seen by many as the fundamental test for the appropriateness of these systems. Nonetheless, there remains a lack of clarity over what precisely meaningful human control entails.

A Commonsense Conception of Control

In his classic discussion of free will and responsibility Daniel Dennett defines control as follows: '*A controls B* if and only if the relations between *A* and *B* is such that *A* can *drive B* into whichever of *B*'s normal range of states *A* wants *B* to be in' (Dennett 1984, 52).

This is, of course, a philosopher's definition of control. But on closer inspection it becomes clear that Dennett is in fact simply articulating how most people, if they paused to think about it, would define control. In everyday language the claim here is that the prerequisites for an agent to have control over something are that the agent (a) has *intentions* about the state or behaviour of that thing, and (b) the *ability* to cause the thing in question to go into the intended state or to behave in the intended way.

To illustrate, let us imagine that I am in a room that is colder than I would like it to be. There is a heater in the room, I desire to be warmer, and so I form the intention that the heater should begin to generate heat in order to raise the temperature in the room. I will have control over the heater if (and only if) (a) I have some *intention* about the state of the heater (which I do – I intend that it generate heat, which is within its normal range of states), and (b) I have the *ability* to cause the heater to go into the intended state. For the latter requirement, let us imagine that the heater is operated by a very simple on–off switch. As I am physically able to manipulate the switch, and there is nothing in the environment preventing me from doing so, we may say that, all else being equal, I am in a position to be in control of the heater. On the other hand, if it were the case that I could not access the heater – if, say, it were located inside a locked cabinet, or if its on–off switch has broken off – I would not be in control of the device.

This reveals that an important corollary of the second prerequisite is that the agent must have the *knowledge* necessary to be able to affect the state or behaviour of the thing that is being controlled. Returning to our example, imagine that I am feeling cold, and am aware of the existence of the heater

(I have felt its warmth on a previous visit to the room), but I cannot find any mechanism by which to activate or deactivate the device. Unbeknownst to me, the on–off switch has been disguised as a small figurine located on the table in front of me. Here I have what Dennett (1984, 116) calls a *bare opportunity*: if I had the necessary knowledge I could drive the device into the state I intend it to be in, but I do not have the necessary knowledge. Let us call this requirement for control the requirement of *knowing how*.

A lack of knowledge can also affect control in another way. Imagine this time that the whereabouts and the functioning of the heater's on–off switch are both known to me and accessible to me. I know that it is a cold day (I have been reliably informed so by the Bureau of Meteorology), and I am also aware that the default setting of the heater is 'off' – that is, not generating any heat. I therefore form the intention to turn the device on to warm the room. However, I suffer from a rare malady which prevents me from physically sensing changes in temperature. There is, furthermore, no gauge on the heater to provide me with visual information in this regard. I am also aware that the heater's on–off switch works only intermittently. In this case, let us imagine that the on–off switch is in fact working, and when I manipulate the switch the heater begins to generate heat and the room begins to warm. While my intention has in fact been fulfilled, and as a direct causal result of my intentional actions, there is at least *some* sense in which I do not have everything I want from control – because I have no idea whether or not I have achieved the intended end state. Following Dennett's notion of a 'bare opportunity' we might call this 'bare control'. In many cases it may be sufficient for me to be able to assume that the end state of my actions has been achieved, thereby allowing me to plan and act accordingly, however in other circumstances my not being aware of whether or not I have caused the thing in question to go into the state I intend might be more problematic. Let us call this additional epistemic requirement for having everything we want from control the requirement of *knowing that*. It is worth noting that while *knowing that* will often be important to me, it does not impact on my *responsibility* for the act in question – if I have intentionally caused something to be in some state, I am responsible for that thing being in that state regardless of whether or not I am aware of whether that outcome has been achieved. A boy who throws a rock at a distant window, and runs away before it hits its target, and who also has reason to doubt the accuracy of his throw, is nonetheless responsible for the broken window even if he is out of sight and hearing at the moment the rock shatters the glass (that is, even if he does not *know that* he has broken the window).

Control is never *absolute* for non-omnipotent beings – there are always some factors which cannot be controlled. In seeking to achieve my goal that the heater should generate more heat in order to warm the room, I have no control over such things as the rate of energy transfer between the heater and the air in the room, or the effect of gravity on my arm as I lift it to manipulate the heater's on–off switch. This does not, however, remove the possibility of *effective* control. As Dennett (1984, 54) points out, '[f]oreknowledge is what permits control'. An agent need not be in control of every factor in a particular environment to be able to effectively control something in that environment, so long as the agent can reliably predict the effect each relevant factor will have on the thing in question. While I cannot control the effect of gravity on my arm as I lift it to manipulate the heater's on–off switch, so long as I am (even unconsciously) aware of the amount of energy I must expend in order to lift my arm thus, and so long as there is no unanticipated variation in the earth's gravitational field, I can still drive the device into the intended state. My lack of control extends, of course, to things beyond just the laws of physics. As someone with very little knowledge of the workings of heaters, I have essentially no way to affect the internal functioning of the device. But so long as the device reliably functions in the way I expect it to when I manipulate its on–off switch, I am still able to exercise control over it. *Predictability* is therefore critical to control: the more predictable the environment and the more predictable the functioning of the object of control, the lower the epistemic threshold for effective control.

Control and Intervening Devices

Returning to the imagined scenario with which we started, I am now able to use the on–off switch in order to control the heater in the room and achieve a more comfortable temperature – let us say, an energy-efficient 19° C. This is clearly good (hooray for control!). However, under the current arrangement I must get up and leave my computer each time I want the state of the heater to change: when the heater is on, the temperature in the room will eventually go well above 19°, so it will be too warm and I will need to get up and turn the heater off. Later, with the heater turned off, the temperature will drop below 19°, so I will need to get up again and turn it back on. In the interest of getting my book written, it would be better if I were not required to manipulate the heater's on–off switch constantly and directly.

Imagine, then, that I instead call a heating specialist, who installs a thermostat that interacts with the heater's on–off switch. Out of nostalgia, I ask the heating specialist to install a simple and purely mechanical vintage Honeywell T87 thermostat. As a bimetallic thermostat, the T87 takes advantage of the different rate of expansion and contraction displayed by different metals in response to temperature change so as to mechanically activate or deactivate a heater's on–off switch, as required by the temperature set by the user on a mechanical dial.

How does the installation of the T87 thermostat affect my control of the heater? Clearly the situation still fits our definition of control. I am now *able* to set the thermostat at the temperature I *intend* and to leave the thermostat to mechanically manipulate the heater's on–off switch such that the temperature in the room remains within a degree or two of 19°. (This is because, after all, the simple mechanical thermostat is reactive: the temperature must drop or increase before it manipulates the on–off switch, and a few minutes pass before the increased heat output returns the temperature to 19°.)

In everyday language we would probably refer to this simple thermostat as a 'controller'. But that is inaccurate; as we have seen, control requires having intentions, which is not a quality we would generally ascribe to a mechanical device. Instead, the simple thermostat is a *control mechanism*, a mechanism through which I control the temperature, an *intervening device* that represents the means by which I cause the heater to be in the state I intend it to be.

This example shows that *control and direct manipulation are not synonymous*. While I had an adequate degree of control when I was directly manipulating the heater's on–off switch, adding the intervening mechanism of the simple thermostat increased my control, while at the same time reducing my direct manipulation of the heating system. Of course, intervening mechanisms do not always increase control. If I had added a poor-quality thermostat – say, one that works only intermittently – I would have reduced my level of control. *The impact that intervening devices have on control is contingent on their effectiveness and reliability*. The directness of the means by which the agent seeks to control some object is, likewise, only contingently related to the degree of control. If an intervening mechanism functions ineffectively or unreliably, then direct manipulation could well increase the degree of control, while if the intervening mechanism works very well then direct manipulation may decrease the level of control.

Does the nature of the intervening device make a fundamental difference? What if I had instead asked the heating specialist to install an electric rather than a mechanical thermostat? It is hard to see why that would change things much; the electric thermostat would still be a control mechanism, and its impact on my control would be contingent on its effectiveness. But what if the engineer installs a sophisticated, algorithm-enabled 'smart' thermostat like the Nest Learning Thermostat, which learns my daily schedule and temperature preferences after a few weeks of my manipulating the system manually, and then adjusts the output of the heating and cooling device predictively, removing the requirement for me to directly manipulate the system? The smart thermostat also uses sensors in the house, as well as the global positioning system (GPS) location of my phone, to switch to energy-saving mode when I am not home, but warms the house to my preferred temperature when it detects that I am approaching the house. This would certainly be a far more sophisticated mechanism than the simple mechanical thermostat, but there seems no reason to see it as being different in principle. The intervening device is still a control mechanism, no different in principle from its simpler cousins, and its impact on my control would be contingent on its effectiveness and reliability and on my own understanding of what is required to make the device fulfil my intentions – in other words, my *knowing how*.[9]

---

[9] In his book *Army of None*, Paul Scharre reports his own experience with a Nest Learning Thermostat: 'There were bumps along the way as I discovered various aspects of the Nest's functionality and occasionally the house was temporarily too warm or too cold ... My wife, Heather, was less tolerant of the Nest [than I was]. Every time it changed the temperature on its own, disregarding an instruction she had given, she viewed it more and more suspiciously. (Unbeknownst to her, the Nest was following other guidance I had given it previously.) The final straw for the Nest was when we came home from summer vacation to find the house a toasty 84 degrees, despite my having gone online the night before and set the Nest to a comfortable 70. ... As it turned out, I had neglected to turn off the 'auto-away feature'. After the Nest's hallway sensor detected no movement and discerned we were not home, it reverted – per its programming – to the energy-saving 'away' setting of 84 degrees. One look from Heather told me it was too late, though. She had lost trust in the Nest. (Or, more accurately, in my ability to use it.)' (Sharre 2018, 33). The parenthetical addendum is important: the problem here was not that the Nest system is autonomous, the problem was with Sharre's knowledge of how to operate the system to achieve his intentions. In the terminology I have used here, it is a problem of knowing how.

A fundamental difference would perhaps occur if the heating specialist installed a machine that had reached a level of artificial general intelligence (AGI) such that we might reasonably consider it to be an agent. However, since it is controversial whether this will ever be achieved and AGI is not part of the most accepted definition of autonomous weapons, let us set that debate aside.

There is more that could be said in articulating a commonsense conception of control, but we have enough here to be able to consider the application of this general one to the specific case of LAWS, for the purpose of better understanding the notion of meaningful human control.

Control and LAWS

Let us begin by redirecting our thoughts from thermostats to the world of military weapon systems. Among the simplest of military weapons is the *mortar* – an indirect fire weapon consisting of a muzzle-loaded smooth-bore tube, generally mounted on a baseplate and supported by a bipod or similar device, from which projectiles are launched using a chemical propellant. Imagine, then, a soldier on a contemporary battlefield employing a mortar.

To keep the scenario as simple as possible, imagine that the weapon system is a small 60 mm patrol mortar that is entirely operated by the soldier in question. While other members of her patrol help to ensure the supply of mortar bombs necessary to keep the system 'fed', our soldier is solely responsible for aiming, firing and otherwise employing the weapon system. Let's call the first version of this scenario mortarman 1.

In mortarman 1, the mortarman (as operators of mortars are still known in US service, regardless of their gender) and her patrol receive a request for indirect fire support from a friendly unit in the area that is taking fire from an antiquated, but still potentially deadly, enemy BMP-1 infantry fighting vehicle (IFV). Because the vehicle is well camouflaged, the other unit is able to give only an approximate account of its location, but this rough grid reference falls (just) within the approximately 3.5 km range of our mortarman's 60 mm mortar, which is located out of sight of the firefight, on the other side of an intervening ridge. As an indirect fire weapon, the 60 mm mortar is able to reach over the ridge and, while the BMP-1 is armoured, a direct hit from one of the 60 mm mortar bombs could possibly breach the vehicle's thinner top armour. The main effect of the 60 mm mortar barrage will likely be to kill or wound any dismounted infantry adjacent to the BMP-1 and to degrade the effectiveness of the BMP-1's fire, enabling the friendly unit to withdraw out of range.

Unfortunately, no unmanned aerial vehicle (UAV) or other 'eyes on' aerial platform and no dedicated forward observer on the ground are available for reconnaissance of the target area. Noting that the area in which the firefight is taking place is known to be unpopulated, and seeing that no buildings or transportation routes are marked on the map of the area, our mortarman's patrol commander decides that mortar fire can be employed within the bounds of the requirements of the principle of discrimination and that the use of force that is being considered is both necessary and proportional. Our mortarman is therefore ordered to lay down indirect fire covering a circle with the radius of 100 m around the approximate grid reference for the location of the BMP-1 that the other unit has provided. Following her training, our mortarman calculates the trajectories required to lob her bombs into the target area, adjusts her initial firing solution to account for the prevailing wind and the atmospheric conditions at this altitude, and sets the aiming system on the 60 mm mortar accordingly. She then commences firing at a steady rate of 20 rounds per minute, making small adjustments to her aiming system at intervals, to ensure as best she can that the entire 100-metre target area is saturated.

What shall we say about our mortarman's control in this situation? As a well-trained mortarman, she has the know-how that is necessary for exercising control over the bombs she is launching. She has more than a mere opportunity to exercise control. Of course there are many elements in the environment that she has no control over: she cannot control the effects of gravity on her bombs, or the effect of weather conditions such as winds and atmospheric pressure, or the rate and consistency of burn of the mortar bombs' propellant, and so on. Still, as long as all these elements are sufficiently predictable, it is reasonable to hold that our mortarman has the ability to cause her bombs to be in the state she wants them to be (i.e. flying in a particular direction, at a particular elevation, in order to hit within a particular target area), and that she is therefore in control of them. The 60 mm mortar is an area-effect weapon system; but, noting that reasonable care has been taken to ensure that the area being targeted is highly likely to be free of non-combatants, we can add that she is exercising *responsible* control in the circumstances. She is exercising what we might call the morally appropriate degree of control, which is, in my view, a better description of what we want here than meaningful human control. As is often the case with the use of indirect-fire weapons, in this particular situation our mortarman does not know for sure, at the time her bombs start landing, that her attempts to exert control have been successful. In the terms we used earlier, she does not have *knowledge that*. The bombs are landing on the other side of the ridge, so she cannot see where they land. Furthermore, the noise of the firefight and the distance involved make it impossible to tell whether the bombs are exploding at all, and the friendly unit in contact is too busy trying to disengage from the enemy to be able to report back on their effect. If the wind on the other side were not as she expected, or if the propellant driving the mortar bombs from her mortar tube were defective and burned at a slower or faster rate than expected, or if her sighting system were malfunctioning, her bombs would be flying *out of control*. But, as it happens, the bombs land within the target area and have the intended effect. Because our mortarman does not know that, she has only *bare control*, but is nonetheless responsible for the destruction that her bombs cause.

In mortarman 1, the mortarman exercises control through direct manipulation. She physically sets the mortar's aiming system and physically adjusts the orientation of the mortar tube to launch her bombs at the angle of elevation and in the direction that she intends. There is no more direct way in which to exercise control over a mortar weapon system. Today this basic direct manipulation approach to aiming is, for many types of weapons, being replaced by more sophisticated means of ensuring that munitions strike their target. GPS-guided munitions, for example, are now common.[10] We could therefore reasonably change our scenario to a near-future conflict in which this technology is sufficiently small and inexpensive to allow production of GPS-guided 60 mm mortar bombs. In this amended scenario, mortarman 2, our mortarman is acting in the same manner and under the same conditions as in the first scenario, with one significant exception. In this second case, after the circular 100-metre target area has been entered into the mortar's targeting computer, the computer assigns a spread of precise GPS coordinates to the 20 mortar bombs to be fired, using an algorithm designed to optimize the combined effect of the barrage. Once launched,

[10] The XM395 Precision Guided 120 mm Mortar Munition and the M982 Excalibur GPS guided artillery round are two current examples of guided indirect-fire munitions that are not missiles.

each of these bombs uses its on-board computer to continuously calculate its own trajectory, and the computer further manipulates tiny motors to change the angle of the bomb's fins to steer the bomb precisely onto its preprogrammed target. By doing so, the GPS guidance system is usually able to counteract the effects of sudden gusts of wind, unexpected movement in the mortar tube during launch, or other environmental changes. As the bomb has no inbuilt propulsion system, however, there are limits to this ability to adjust the bomb's trajectory. Consequently, if the on-board computer calculates that it will not be able to steer the bomb onto its programmed target coordinates, the bomb will self-detonate at a safe altitude, minimizing the potential for collateral harm. As in mortarman 1, the bombs strike their intended target and, once again, our mortarman is not informed of the outcome of the strike as it happens.

Clearly in mortarman 2 what has changed is that we have introduced into the situation an *intervening device*, a *control mechanism* that reduces or removes the mortarman's direct manipulation of the weapons system. Does the introduction of the intervening control mechanism reduce the mortarman's control? It's hard to see why this would be so. Through the employment of the computerized GPS guidance system – assuming that it is reliable – our mortarman is still able to *cause* the bombs to strike the target she *intends* them to strike, thereby fulfilling our definition of control. In fact, the very reason for introducing the intervening control mechanism is to increase the degree of control available to the mortarman. If the mechanism works as advertised, it reduces the possibility that factors beyond the mortarman's control will cause the mortar bombs to spin out of control. Of course, if the mechanism is faulty or unreliable, our mortarman may well have more control if she sticks with the traditional direct manipulation method of aiming her bombs. Her degree of control is thus contingent on the reliability and effectiveness (trustworthiness) of the intervening control mechanism. Her degree of control is also contingent on her knowledge of how to operate the system. If she has not been trained to use the new version of the mortar with the computerized GPS guidance system (that is, if she lacks the necessary *knowledge how*), and if its operation is not sufficiently straightforward that she can be justifiably confident that her mortar bombs will land where she intends, she will probably have more control, again, if she relies instead on the direct manipulation backup sighting system, which she knows how to operate effectively.

What of the decision to kill? Our mortarman did not specify precisely where each bomb should land, as she did, to the best of her ability, in mortarman 1. Instead the computerized GPS guidance system assigned a specific, algorithm-generated and geographically defined target to each bomb launched, in a pattern designed to optimize the combined effect of the barrage. Our mortarman did not (and could not) steer the bombs, as she might have done if they were remote-controlled rather than purely GPS-guided. In each individual case, the on-board computer manipulated the bomb's fins in accordance with its programming, in order to ensure that the bomb struck the precise point assigned to it. Do these intervening factors mean that the weapon system itself made the decision to kill? That is quite clearly not the case. We may debate whether the decision to kill was made by our mortarman or by her commander, or whether it was distributed between the two of them (and perhaps others further up the chain of command), but it seems obviously bizarre to consider the workings of the GPS-guided weapons system to be somehow involved in the decision to kill. Yet note that, once our mortarman has entered into the computer the parameters of the attack, the system operates without further human intervention.

It is also worth noting what impact the availability of the GPS-guided bombs has on our mortarman's accountability for the outcomes of her action. Where in mortarman 1 she might have been forgiven if one or more of her bombs had landed outside the area that was targeted, the availability of the GPS-guided bombs (assuming that they work as advertised) means that there is now a greater burden of responsibility for the outcomes. The introduction of the intervening control mechanism has in no way decreased our mortarman's responsibility; on the contrary, it has increased it, and she can reasonably be held accountable as a result.

Let us now consider a final version of this scenario. In this version, mortarman 3, the situation is in all relevant respects the same as in mortarman 1, except that our mortarman turns to an even more technologically advanced capability that is available to her: a system that – even given the ongoing debate on what constitutes an 'autonomous' weapons system – most analysts would be comfortable identifying as a LAWS. Specifically, among her mix of GPS-guided and 'dumb' mortar bombs, she has two algorithm-enabled anti-armour loitering munitions. This small unmanned aerial system is 'popped' from a 60 mm mortar tube, but has an in-built propulsion system that gives it the ability to fly to and circle over a 'geofenced' target location selected by the operator before its launch. Once over the target location, the LAWS employs its miniaturized sensors to seek out vehicles that have signatures that match those in the library of enemy armoured fighting vehicles in its database. On identifying such a vehicle, the LAWS dives onto its target, contact-detonating a shaped warhead designed specifically to penetrate the upper armour of an armoured vehicle and to kill or disable the crew inside. Once launched, the LAWS does this entirely in accordance with the programming of its algorithm and without further intervention from the operator (let us stipulate that the tight dimensions of the 60 mm mortar tube mean that it is not possible to incorporate a video or other feedback or control system that can be manipulated by the operator, so it cannot be remotely controlled or recalled once launched). If a vehicle matching the parameters of an enemy armoured vehicle is not detected, the LAWS will continue loitering until its fuel is exhausted or until a preset time period has elapsed, at which point it will self-destruct at a safe altitude, in order to minimize the possibility of collateral damage and to keep its technology from falling into enemy hands. In this case, our mortar-man opts to launch both LAWS, and both identify and strike the BMP-1 as designed.

What, then, shall we say about mortarman 3? Here we see a system that clearly fits with the ICRC definition of an autonomous weapons system: it 'can select (i.e. search for or detect, identify, track, select) and attack (i.e. use force against, neutralize, damage or destroy) targets without human intervention'. So what are the implications of this 'autonomy' for meaningful human control? Again, so long as the AI-enabled loitering munitions are reliable, it seems hard to say that our mortarman is not in control. She has *intentions* about what the munitions will do, and she is *able* to cause them to do what she wants them to do. Even better, in this case the mortarman's intentions can be more specific: rather than simply intending that the warheads explode within a specified geographic area, she can now specify that each warhead explodes on contact with the upper part of a vehicle that matches key criteria that identify it as an enemy armoured vehicle, or else that it explodes relatively harmlessly, in the sky, if no vehicle matching those criteria is identified. Of course, her control does have limits. As we have stipulated, once the LAWS has been launched, the mortarman no longer has the ability to directly manipulate the munition. But this is also true in the scenarios described in mortarman 1 and mortarman 2. We do not think, it seems to me, that the degree of control the mortarman exercises in mortarman 1 and mortarman 2 is below the morally appropriate degree of control for those circumstances. The degree of control exercised by our mortarman in mortarman 3 is, if anything, greater than in the first two scenarios – it is certainly not less. Yet opponents of LAWS contend that the circumstances described in mortarman 3 and similar circumstances that involve the employment of LAWS fail to meet the requirement of meaningful human control. Why is that?

One answer seems to be that control has been confused with direct manipulation. But, as we have seen, these are not one and the same, and the question of whether direct manipulation increases or decreases control is a contingent one. If the LAWS in mortarman 3 is able to identify enemy armoured vehicles with a very high degree of accuracy, then the algorithm-enabled mechanism that has been mated to the explosive munition and launched from the mortar tube is an intervening device – a control mechanism – that provides our mortarman with a greater degree of control than she would have without it. On the other hand, if the LAWS were unreliable and prone to striking inappropriate targets (that is, if it were untrustworthy), then our mortarman would have decreased control should she choose to use the system, and she would be well advised (operationally, ethically and legally) to stick to a simpler munition and exert a greater degree of direct manipulation. Likewise, if our mortarman did not have the necessary *knowledge how* in relation to operating the system, then again she will have reduced her degree of control in comparison to that of the more basic mortar weapons system of mortarman 1.

Another part of the problem here is that there is a conceptual error that runs through much of the debate. The error is illustrated in the ICRC's articulation of what it sees as 'the fundamental question at the heart of ethical discussions' of this topic: 'whether, irrespective of compliance with international law, the principles of humanity and the dictates of the public conscience can allow human decision-making on the use of force to be effectively substituted with computer controlled processes, and life-and-death decisions to be *ceded* to machines' (ICRC 2018, 4–5, italics added). Similarly, HRW contends that using LAWS amounts to '[c]*eding* human control over decisions about who lives and who dies' (Human Rights Watch 2016, 3, italics added). The problem with these statements is that a controller cannot cede control to a control mechanism; a controller can cede control only to another controller. In mortarman 3 our mortarman does not cede control to the LAWS loitering munitions she launches from her tube, *she employs those munitions as a means to exert control.* Whether she does so successfully depends, as we have said, on how reliably the LAWS does what she wants it to do and on whether she has sufficient knowledge to be justifiably confident in operating the system. If the system is unreliable and does something unexpected, unintended or inappropriate (such as, say, homing in on a civilian vehicle some distance from the geofenced area it has been launched at), or if the system is reliable but is operated without the necessary know-how and has such consequences, then the problem is not that our mortarman has ceded control to the LAWS. The problem is that, in using an unreliable control mechanism or in using a control mechanism she does not know how to operate effectively, she has failed to exercise the morally appropriate degree of control and would be responsible – and could be held accountable – for the effects of choosing that munition, just as she would be responsible – and could be held accountable – for opting to use any of the other munitions available to her.

This notion that employing LAWS entails *ceding* control is also reflected in worries that employing

LAWS threatens the dignity of those at the receiving end. As the ICRC contends, '[i]t is argued that, if human agency is lacking to the extent that machines have effectively, and functionally, been *delegated* [decisions to kill, injure and destroy], then it undermines the *human dignity* of those combatants targeted, and of civilians that are put at risk as a consequence of legitimate attacks on military targets' (ICRC 2018, 2, italics added). Similarly, according to HRW, '[c]*eding* human control over decisions about who lives and who dies would deprive people of their inherent *dignity*' (Human Rights Watch 2016, italics added). But is this in fact the case? In the next chapter we consider whether questions of motives and dignity might be sufficient to justify a ban on 'killer robots'.

4

Motives and Dignity

Reflecting a strongly held view among opponents of lethal autonomous weapons systems (LAWS), the Holy See (2015) has claimed that these systems would be – like mass rape campaigns and the use of poisonous gas – *mala in se* ('evils in themselves'). Why? Because, it is argued, allowing a weapon system to choose whether or not to kill human beings (and *which* human beings to kill) is a violation of human dignity. But is that so? And what, exactly, is the basis for that claim?

Dignity and 'Ceding'

Among the more sophisticated attempts to articulate the basis for what we might call 'the dignity objection'[11] to LAWS is the claim, advanced by

[11] As one Twitter pundit put it, 'it's about the dignity, stupid'.

Michael Skerker and his co-authors, Duncan Purves and Ryan Jenkins, that

> service personnel cede a right not to be directly targeted with lethal violence to other human agents alone. Artificial agents, of which AWS [autonomous weapons systems] are one example, cannot understand the value of human life. A human combatant cannot transfer his privileges of targeting enemy combatants to a robot. Therefore, the human duty-holder who deploys AWS breaches the martial contract between human combatants and disrespects the targeted combatants. (Skerker et al. 2020)

(For the purposes of our discussion, autonomous weapons systems are practically equivalent with LAWS.) Skerker and his colleagues cleverly place the argument in the context of the concept of the moral equality of combatants – a powerful, albeit contested (Barry and Christie 2018) concept in the just war tradition. However, the concern is in essence the same as the one expressed, as we saw, by the ICRC and the Human Rights Watch. It is a concern over ceding or delegating a human responsibility to a LAWS.

But, as argued in the previous chapter, this fundamentally misrepresents the relationship between the human operator and the LAWS. Consider again our earlier thought experiment. In mortarman 3, the idea that the decision to kill has been 'delegated' or 'ceded' to the LAWS is erroneous, because the LAWS is a control mechanism, not a controller. To put it another way, it is not – as Skerker et al. (2020) would have it – an 'agent'. The decision to kill has been made by our mortarman (or by her commanding officer, or by some combination of the two, or is distributed through the chain of command), and the LAWS has applied the parameters set by her. A comparison between mortarman 2 and mortarman 3 is instructive in this regard. In mortarman 2, remember, the GPS-guided system employs a simple algorithm to saturate a defined area of ground with mortar fire. The parameters applied in this case are geographical. In mortarman 3, geographical parameters are also applied (the area in which the LAWS is operational is geofenced with the help of GPS data), but additional parameters defined by such things as the visual, thermal, magnetic and acoustic signature typical of vehicles of a certain type are added as further constraints. If the LAWS identifies a target that falls within these parameters and its on-board navigational system thus steers it into the upper armour of an enemy armoured vehicle, the LAWS in question has no more *choice* in the matter and has made no more of a *decision* to do what it does than the GPS-guided munition in mortarman 2, when it lands on the spot designated by the area-saturation algorithm. Again, the LAWS is not an agent or a controller. Unless there is some intrinsic difference between an algorithm that steers a weapon according to geographic data and one that steers a weapon according to visual, thermal, magnetic or acoustic data (or some combination of these), there is no fundamental difference between mortarman 2 and mortarman 3. To speak of LAWS as making the decision to kill is to anthropomorphize LAWS and at the same time to play fast and loose with language. And if a LAWS has not made the decision to kill, then it is nonsensical to speak of the human operator as having somehow 'ceded' or 'delegated' that decision to the LAWS.

Motives

Even if we were willing (as I am not) to grant that something important has been ceded or delegated to the LAWS, this dignity objection rests on another important confusion, namely over the role that *motives* should play in warfare. Here again it is useful to consider the two analogies I have been drawing on: contracted combatants (the figurative dogs of war) and weaponized animals (the literal dogs of war).

As I explored in *Just Warriors, Inc.*, perhaps the biggest objection to the employment of contracted combatants relates to their motivation. The worry is that either they are motivated by the wrong things – things they ought not to be motivated by, such as blood lust or a love of filthy lucre above all else (what Tony Lynch and A. J. Walsh 2000 call 'lucrepathology') – or they lack the kind of motivation that is appropriate for engaging in war – for example impelled by the just cause or by recognition of the moral equality of combatants. Clearly in the case of contracted combatants it does seem meaningful to speak of the employer 'ceding' or 'delegating' to these people the decision to kill. Contracted combatants are agents or controllers in the relevant sense. So, if we were (mistakenly) to find an analogous relationship between the human operator and a LAWS, then the problem would look very similar. To put this objection in the terms used by Lynch and Walsh (2000, 138), 'justifiable killing motives must . . . include just cause and right intention', and because these are not motives an autonomous weapons system is capable of (being incapable of having motives at all), it is concluded that the dignity of those on the receiving end is violated.

Part of the problem with this objection, applied to both contracted combatants and autonomous weapons systems, is that it seems to take an unrealistic view of motivation among military personnel engaged in war. It would be bizarre to claim that every member of a national military force was motivated by the desire to satisfy the nation's just cause in fighting a war, or by a recognition of the moral equality of combatants; and even those who are motivated by these values are unlikely to be motivated in this way in every instance of combat. If the lack of such a motive results in dignity violations to the extent that the situation is ethically untenable, then what we have here is an argument against war in general, not a specific argument against the employment of mercenaries or autonomous weapons systems.

The motive or dignity objection overlooks an important distinction, namely that between intention and motive. James Pattison explains:

An individual's *intention* is the objective or purpose that they wish to achieve with their action. On the other hand, their *motive* is their underlying reason for acting. It follows that an agent with right intention aims to tackle whatever it is that the war is a just response to, such as a humanitarian crisis, military attack, or serious threat. But their underlying reason for having this intention need not also concern the just cause. It could be, for instance, a self-interested reason. (Pattison 2010, 147)

Or, we might add – given that autonomous weapons systems do not have intrinsic *reasons* for what they do – it could be no reason at all. Consider again the example of combat assault dogs. Whatever motives they may have in engaging enemy targets (or in selecting one target over another), it seems safe to say that 'achieving the just cause' or 'recognizing the moral equality of combatants' is not among them. But the lack of a general, dignity-based outcry against using combat assault dogs to cause harm to the enemy points to a widely held intuition that what matters here is that the dogs' actions are in accord with appropriate *intentions* on the part of the handler and the military force that handler belongs to.

Or consider once again, as a thought experiment, B. F. Skinner's pigeon-guided munition (PGM), which we encountered in chapter 1. Imagine that, after his initial success (let's call it PGM-1), Skinner had gone one step further. Rather than being trained just to steer the bomb onto one particular ship (identified by the pilot of the launching aircraft), the pigeons had been trained to be able to pick out the most desirable target from a range of enemy ships that appear on their tiny screen: they have learned to recognize and rank aircraft carriers above battleships, battleships above cruisers, cruisers above destroyers and so on. They have been trained to then direct their bomb onto the most desirable target that is within the range of its glide path. What Skinner would have created, in this fictional case, is an autonomous weapon that employs 'organic control' (ORCON). We might even call it an AI-directed autonomous weapon (where 'AI' stands for 'animal intelligence'). Let's call this weapon system 'pigeon-guided munition 2' (PGM-2). Because the pigeons in PGM-1 act only as a steering mechanism and do not 'decide' either to attack the ship or *which* ship to attack, the motive argument clearly does not apply, and therefore we can conclude that those killed and injured in the targeted ship did not have their dignity violated. But supporters of the dignity objection would have to say that anyone killed or injured in a ship targeted by a PGM-2 rather than by a PGM-1 has also suffered a dignity violation. Indeed, if we apply the Holy See's position on autonomous weapons systems to this case, we would have to say that using a PGM-2 in war amounts to employing means that are *mala in se*, which is equivalent to employing poisonous gas, rape as a weapon of war, or torture. But this is patently absurd.

The Awkwardness of the Dignity Objection

There is another reason to be leery of the dignity objection. In what remains of this chapter I want to highlight just how *awkward* this objection is. Of course, it doesn't look that way on the surface. For many of us in the contemporary West the idea that humans have a fundamental dignity is part of what the Canadian philosopher Charles Taylor calls our 'social imaginary': 'that common understanding which makes possible common practices, and a widely shared sense of legitimacy' (Taylor 2007, 172). As a consequence, the idea of human dignity 'has come to count as the taken-for-granted shape of things, too obvious to mention' (Taylor 2004, 22).

One response to the dignity objection to the use of LAWS is to challenge, as I have just done, the claim that employing LAWS actually undermines this unearned worth or status of humans in some way that employing other weapons of war does not. Others might object to the application of such a distinctly western and individualistic ethical concept as the basis for a global effort to rule out the use of LAWS. It is noteworthy, for example, that the written submissions made by the delegation from China to the UN Group of Governmental Experts tasked with evaluating this issue incorporate essentially all the objections outlined in the ICRC report *except* the dignity objection (Baker forthcoming).

But my goal here is not to directly challenge the dignity objection, only to highlight its awkwardness. Even if we accept as a given that LAWS will violate human dignity when they kill someone, in practice such violations will often, and perhaps usually, be *invisible*. It seems likely that military forces will generally prefer weapons systems that are not always autonomous but are instead optionally autonomous – that is to say, systems that can operate autonomously but can also be remotely operated by a human operator. If I am right about this, then it will often be difficult or impossible for an external observer to tell whether the system is operating autonomously or is being operated by a human being. Accordingly, when someone is killed by such a system – let's say, by an 'uninhabited' but 'optionally autonomous' armed aerial vehicle – we will be in the very awkward position of having to say that that person's dignity *might* have been violated, but we just don't know. S*omeone* will know – the person who makes the decision as to whether the machine's switch is flipped to autonomous mode or not – but for everyone else the dignity violation will be invisible.

Of course, a right *can* be violated without anyone but the perpetrator knowing about it. The peeping Tom who never gets caught nonetheless is still a violator of his victim's right to privacy. The idea that a human's dignity is violated if he or she is killed by a LAWS is not *negated* by the invisibility of that violation. Still, when invisible violations are potentially the most common cases, the situation is at least very awkward. An invisible dignity violation is an uncomfortably ethereal basis for regulating as crude and base a practice as the use of violence in war. If we want to walk down this path, we should at least do so with our eyes open to how different this perspective is from the existing constraints on military force. The laws and ethics of war focus almost exclusively on limiting the infliction of physical harm and suffering; they are a humanitarian but pragmatic response to a decidedly non-ideal form of human interaction. As Valerie Morkevičius has shown in her excellent book on the just war tradition, attempts to base an ethics of war on exquisite ideals are anomalous in relation to the broad sweep of that tradition and, more importantly, almost inevitably end up effectively in a position of pacifism. That may be fine in a philosopher's study, but it will not do for the real world. We need rugged and realistic rules that self-interested states might actually abide by. 'When the rules are pragmatic – when they reflect the ways wars are fought and won – they are more likely to be obeyed. At the very least, a common excuse for overriding the rules has been eliminated' (Morkevičius 2018, 225).

The Dignity Argument and Strongly Held Intuitions

I am not so naïve as to think that the arguments in this chapter will convince opponents to change their position. Arguments are weak beer in comparison with deeply held moral intuitions, and it seems to me entirely conceivable that this is an issue on which people may simply have irreconcilable moral intuitions.

This was brought home to me forcefully at a 2018 meeting of the International Panel for the

Regulation of Autonomous Weapons (IPRAW).[12] The Panel, of which I was then a member, had previously met five times and addressed a range of topics relevant to autonomous weapons, in line with its mandate of 'supporting the current debate within the UN CCW with scientifically grounded information and recommendations' (IPRAW n.d.). This was the first meeting explicitly focused on ethics and, as one of the panel's ethicists, I played a role in facilitating the discussion.

One of the sessions of that meeting made a particular impression on me. I was leading it, using the mortarman scenarios outlined in chapter 3 of this volume as a way to draw out the panel members' intuitions on the topic. Things proceeded as I had imagined they would until we got to mortarman 3. This is where the rubber hit the road, so to speak. How would the panellists respond? Having designed the thought experiment, I fully expected that my co-panellists would share my intuitions, as they had for mortarman 1 and mortarman 2. Specifically, I expected that they would agree with me that adding

---

[12] The IPRAW was jointly organized by the German Institute for International and Security Affairs (Stiftung Wissenschaft und Politik) and the Johns Hopkins University Applied Physics Laboratory (JHU APL), and was financially supported by the German Federal Foreign Office.

further targeting parameters (defined by the visual, thermal, magnetic, acoustic, etc. signature of vehicles of a certain type) to the algorithm-processed geographic targeting parameters that were present in mortarman 2 would not change the ethical valence of the situation beyond the positive effect of increasing precision and reducing the overall destructiveness of the strike. In this, however, I was very much mistaken. While several panellists did share my intuition, several others reported that their strongly held moral intuition was that an ethical Rubicon had been crossed, and that the scenario in mortarman 3 represents a violation of the human dignity of those targeted in the strike. Despite a vigorous (but respectful!) discussion around the table, it soon became clear that these opposing views were irreconcilable: no amount of argument or reasoning would result in agreement.

I doubt that this experience is unique. In fact, I am now convinced that deeply held and ultimately irreconcilable moral intuitions are the primary reason why it has proven so difficult to reach an agreement on whether we should ban killer robots. In the face of this deeply held and perhaps insurmountable difference of moral opinion, what should one do? If it were up to me, I would reject the idea of a ban. But, of course, this is exactly the point: it is *not* up to me. Indeed, this is not a decision for individuals at all, whichever way our particular moral intuitions may lean. Nor is it a decision that should be based (in a liberal democracy at least) on any particular religious authority, for instance by following the Holy See's declaration that the use of LAWS constitutes a *malum in se*. It is a decision made at the level of states. So, then, what should states do when a method or means of war is ethically controversial, but there is no clear consensus on the matter?

One option is for policymakers to feel justified in ignoring the controversy and to simply choose whichever side of the debated issue best fits with the state's responsibility to protect its citizens. Following this logic, it seems that states that are likely to be in a position to make use of LAWS should enthusiastically embrace them, because such systems seem very likely to offer both a military advantage and a means to keep members of the state's armed forces out of harm's way. On the other hand, states that can foresee that they will be militarily disadvantaged by the introduction of autonomous weapons to the battlefield (because, for example, they are unlikely to be able to afford them) will have a strong reason to push for an international ban on such weapons, as a way to try to prevent at least some potential adversaries from being advantaged by this capability.

But this 'solution' won't do. For one thing, it simply boils down to self-interest on the part of the state. For another, it provides no basis for international consensus on how to move forward on this issue: states that think they would benefit militarily from autonomous weapons will push for their use, while states that think they would be losers if autonomous weapons are used will push for a ban, and there will be an international impasse that cannot be resolved on principle. Furthermore, such a solution gives short shrift to the real and important fact that there is significant moral controversy on this issue among the state's citizens, even when the state itself in practice takes up a position, albeit on pragmatic grounds. So the quandary remains. Adopting some policy position on autonomous weapons is ultimately unavoidable for states and policymakers, but in the absence of a clear ethical consensus any decision appears to be either base pragmatism or an inappropriate substitution of the policymaker's personal moral intuitions for the position of the state.

In *Citizen Killings* (Baker 2016) I address a range of structurally similar ethical quandaries for policymakers. Bearing in mind that liberal states have a responsibility to protect the right to life under the social contract and that the principle of liberal neutrality means that liberal states generally ought not to adopt either positions that favour or affirm one conception of the good life over another or the metaphysical commitments that underpin the conception they favour, how are policymakers to decide on appropriate policy when there are strongly held competing views on matters such as what constitutes human life and its violation?[13] To address such situations, I proposed that policymakers must first assess whether the competing views pass what I call the 'reasonableness test':

> The principle is that the state is only under a responsibility to weigh up competing moral conceptions of the kind being addressed here when those conceptions can properly be considered, at the time that the policy is being assessed, to be reasonable. Here I have in mind something broadly akin to the 'reasonable person' test in common law. Whereas in law the question is whether or not a particular act falls short of the test of what a reasonable person might have done in the same circumstances, the test

[13] In Baker (2016) I consider decisions about the appropriateness of brain death or of the traditional standard of cardiopulmonary death as the marker of the end of a life, or about the permissibility of elective abortions.

of reasonableness I am proposing here is whether
or not the claim or position under consideration is
one that could reasonably be believed in the society
in which the policy question is being considered.
(Baker 2016, 55, n11)

The reasonableness test has two parts. First, there
is a requirement that the view under discussion must
have significant support among the population:
policymakers are under no obligation to take into
account moral positions that are not widely supported. Second, there is the requirement that 'the
position or view or claim in question must be the
focus of a significant body of serious and respected
argument put forward in its favour by people recognized in society as intellectually credible (call this
the "intellectual credibility requirement")' (Baker
2016, 55).

There are essentially three competing views on
the dignity objection to LAWS that must be considered. First, there is the view that those who are
targeted (or collaterally harmed) by LAWS have
their human dignity violated as a consequence and
that this is sufficient ground for a ban on LAWS.
Second, there is the opposing view, that the use of
autonomous weapons does not violate anybody's
human dignity. (There are multiple possible bases

for this view, for example the idea that dignity is not a moral feature of human beings, or the idea that the employment of an autonomous weapon does not break the appropriate moral link between the weapon's operator and the victim and dignity is therefore maintained. But the policymaker need not concern herself with these reasons, once it has been established that the contending views are irreconcilable: it is the views themselves that must be considered.) Third, there is the view that the use of autonomous weapons does (or may) violate human dignity but that this is outweighed by other morally relevant factors, such as the potential to save the lives of non-combatants by reducing the risk of collateral damage through the use of these weapons systems.

It seems that we may cautiously conclude that all three of these views meet the reasonableness test. While no study I am aware of has yet investigated public opinion specifically on the question of autonomous weapons and human dignity, more general polling for public opinion on the use of autonomous weapons in war has shown that a significant proportion of the populations polled fall on either side of this question. Notably, a rigorous US study by Michael Horowitz published in 2016 showed that, rather than being staunchly opposed, public attitudes are strongly influenced by context around autonomous weapons. When the lives of US troops are on the line, when AWS may be more effective than alternatives, or when others are developing AWS, opposition reduces. This is consistent with political science research on public opinion, weapons, and war, though contrary to more extreme claims about public opposition to AWS. (Horowitz 2016, 7)

Likewise, a scan of the scholarly literature on the ethics of autonomous weapons shows that there is, in relative terms, 'a significant body of serious and respected argument put forward in its favour by people recognized in society as intellectually credible' (Baker 2016, 55; also quote at p. 102) and that this body of argument is associated, at least broadly, with all three of these views. Thus both the requirement for sufficient support and the requirement for intellectual credibility are met on all these views, and the policymaker is bound to take all three into consideration.

When two or more competing positions over an appropriate policy meet this reasonableness test and a policy position must nonetheless be taken that will inescapably favour one of these positions over the other(s), I argue that states should opt for the least morally risky option available.

Moral Risk and Autonomous Weapons

Specifically, in such situations I argue that policymakers should apply what I call 'the risk of harm principle'. This principle requires the policymaker to take as a starting point the artificial assumption that all the positions involved are correct, and from there to undertake a comparative assessment of how much risk is involved in adopting a policy that goes against each of those positions.

Consider, first, the view that the use of autonomous weapons violates the human dignity of those at the receiving end. Clearly the risk here, in adopting a policy that allows for the use of autonomous weapons, is that human dignity will be violated. Second, what about the opposite view, that autonomous weapons do not violate human dignity? If a policy is adopted that rejects this position, the risk is that states will forego any opportunity to develop a war-fighting capability that could in principle reduce non-combatant deaths and keep some of their own personnel out of harm's way. Third, there is the view that human dignity is or may be violated through the use of autonomous weapons, but that this consideration is outweighed by other morally relevant factors, such as the potential to save the lives of non-combatants through reduced risk of collateral damage when using these weapons systems. If a policy is adopted that in practice rejects this view (e.g. a policy that bans the use of autonomous weapons), the risk is similar to the one presented by the second scenario here, though the weight of the risk is lower because, if this view is correct, then human dignity is preserved by the policy. In this view human dignity matters morally, even if it is outweighed by the lives of non-combatants that would be lost if a ban is imposed.

In essence, then, the policymaker must weigh up the risk of violating human dignity against the risk of death and harm that may befall non-combatants and against the risk of death and harm that may befall some of the state's uniformed service members (those who would be required to serve in the field in order to fulfil roles that would otherwise be carried out by autonomous systems).[14] Both

14 It might be argued that the opportunity to use remotely piloted but unmanned systems renders this moot. This, however, ignores the fact that one of the main operational reasons for turning to autonomous systems is their use in communications-denied environments. Thus, for example, if a military force wishes to destroy a ground target deep in enemy territory during a high-intensity battle in which the enemy is using wide-scale jamming to block communications, such that a remote communications link necessary to pilot an unmanned system is not available, it must either send a manned aircraft or an autonomous system to do the job. Under such circumstances the risk level is likely to be

the right to dignity and the right to life are very weighty, so how shall we compare them? One point to note here is that, if the use of autonomous weapons does violate the right to dignity, in most cases it does so in a somewhat reduced way. That is, when someone is killed by an autonomous weapon, that person will have no sense that her dignity has been violated. The situation is similar to the harm of desecrating a dead body. While this is unquestionably a harm, and one that derives from the core notion of human dignity, it seems more diffuse, and is perhaps about human dignity in general rather than about the particular dignity of the person whose corpse has been desecrated. Notice also that, as I argued in the previous chapter, it is quite possible that, if the use of autonomous weapons does violate human dignity, those violations will in many cases be *invisible*. Given that autonomous and remotely piloted systems will probably appear alongside each other on future battlefields and that many systems will be designed so as to be able to be switched from remotely piloted mode to autonomous mode, there is a very high likelihood that those at the receiving

very high (adversaries with advanced electronic warfare capabilities generally have advanced anti-aircraft systems too), and if autonomous weapons are not allowed the risk will fall on the human pilot.

end will have no idea whether or not their dignity has been violated (and their loved ones will not know either). As we have seen, this does not mean that the victims' dignity has not been violated. But, still, this prospect of invisibility as a regular feature of dignity violations seems to me in this case to reduce the weight of these violations somewhat.

The most compelling point in weighing up the risk of violating the right to dignity against the risk of violating the right to life in this context is also the most obvious one. The right to life is unrecoverable; once an individual has lost her life she cannot regain it. On the other hand, those whose dignity is violated and who survive have the opportunity to recover their dignity or to have it restored to them. Those who die and in the process have their dignity violated as well do not experience any greater harm than those who have only their right to life violated: they are dead, and that is all. Others (family, loved ones, friends and colleagues) may of course experience the harm of that dignity violation, but it seems likely that the dignity of the victim can be regained in the memory of those affected – through acts of remembrance, for example. This extended notion of dignity is, of course, somewhat nebulous and difficult to articulate and address – itself an indication that, for the policymaker, the more concrete idea of a right to life should weigh more heavily.

Ironically, then, it seems that what should guide the policymaker's choice of what is appropriate when considering the deontological question of human dignity is the contingent issues of (1) whether autonomous weapons can in fact be employed in such a way as to reduce the risk of collateral harm to non-combatants and (2) whether they can be used to reduce to a significant degree the risk of harm to uniformed members of the state's armed forces. If they cannot, then the risk of violating human dignity should compel the policymaker to outlaw their use. If, on the other hand, it seems that the use of autonomous weapons could genuinely result in lives saved among non-combatants and own forces, then the right to life trumps the right to dignity in this case.

Conclusion

So Then, Should We Ban Killer Robots?

In this short book I have addressed the core arguments in favour of the claim that we should ban 'killer robots'. Chapter 1 set the scene by showing how these arguments against using the 'robot dogs of war' are in essence the same as those against the use of contracted combatants (the figurative dogs of war) and how they also parallel what we might imagine to be the most forceful arguments against the use of weaponized animals (the real dogs of war). In chapter 2 I considered, and dismissed, the claim that lethal autonomous weapons systems (LAWS) cannot be trusted to operate reliably within the bounds of the ethical and legal constraints that apply to the use of force in armed conflict. Of course *some* LAWS in *some* contexts would be untrustworthy in this regard, but there is nothing intrinsic to LAWS that means that there are not real-world circumstances in which they could be used in compliance with the ethics and laws of war. Chapter 3 focused on the idea of meaningful human control in relation to LAWS. I argued that concerns about control, and therefore account-ability, fundamentally misunderstand the nature of LAWS, mistakenly treating these systems as controllers or agents, when they are in fact control mechanisms. I continued, in chapter 4, by address-ing the dignity objection to LAWS – that is, the idea that employing these systems in combat amounts to a violation of the dignity of those killed by them. Here again I showed that the objection rests on mistaking these control devices for controllers or agents. Furthermore, it depends on a problematic conception of the role of motives in appropriate killing and harm in war. I also argued that dignity is an awkward notion in this context and pointed out how dissimilar the supposed dignity violation inflicted by LAWS is from other means and meth-ods of war that have been deemed *mala in se* (evils in themselves). Nonetheless, I recognize that the issue of LAWS triggers deep-seated moral intuitions that might ultimately be irreconcilable. Against this backdrop, I have proposed a way for states to resolve the issue in line with the foundational prin-ciples that underpin liberalism, and I conclude that the deciding factor is whether we might reasonably expect lethal autonomous weapons to offer a means by which the state can lower the risk of causing collateral damage when justly committing its forces to war, as well as whether these systems offer a means by which to protect the lives of members of that state's armed forces.

In this short volume space does not allow a full evaluation of this final question. The answer, in broad terms, is very much dependent on how well states are able to align the technological capabilities of the LAWS they develop with the contexts and environments in which those systems will be used. In the narrower sense, of course, it is pretty clear that individual systems that exist or will soon exist could well be sufficiently trustworthy (as discussed in chapter 2) to be used appropriately in some environments. Other existing and future systems will, no doubt, not be sufficiently trustworthy, and therefore pose too high a risk of causing 'indiscriminate effects' (ICRC 2021). But we already have international laws that restrict the use of weapons in ways that result in indiscriminate effects; a ban on autonomous weapons would offer little further value, but would deny the opportunity to use these systems in ways that may reduce the destructiveness of war.

While the arguments I have considered in this book are undoubtedly the core arguments raised against LAWS, there are others, which could not be addressed in the space available. For example, there is the question of whether LAWS might threaten trust in a different way from that addressed in chapter 2: do they lower the threshold for the use of force such that they make 'the use of violence easier or less controlled' (ICRC 2018, 9), and thereby undermine our ability to trust policymakers to use force ethically and legally? This is certainly a challenge, but it is not one that is specific to autonomous weapons. Instead, there is the potential that a wide range of military policy tools, both new (cyberwarfare) and old (mercenaries, proxy forces), would tempt policymakers to act in a way that violates the *ius ad bellum* norms of war. Banning autonomous weapons is not the solution to this challenge. This is, instead, an issue that must be addressed by placing appropriate democratic controls on the use of force. It is a problem of governance, not a problem of technology.

Or consider the argument that even states that would benefit militarily from autonomous weapons should oppose their use, on the grounds that the introduction of such weapons would cause strategic instability, which is harmful to all. For example, a 'pledge' hosted by the Future of Life Institute to which thousands of scholars, scientists and organizations have become signatories claims, without further explanation, that 'lethal autonomous weapons, selecting and engaging targets without human intervention, would be dangerously destabilizing for every country and individual' (Future of Life Institute, n.d.). This is a dramatic claim, for which very little evidence actually exists. AI in general will certainly change war as we know it, but this effect will extend far beyond just autonomous weapons. Even if the claim quoted here were true, the assumption is that an international ban on the use of autonomous weapons will stave off this predicted instability. Given that the growth in the use of autonomous systems is expected to be huge in the commercial sector, there seems little likelihood that an international ban will have a significant impact on the development and employment of autonomous weapons systems by rogue regimes and non-state actors. This renders the assumption very problematic indeed.

In our discussions in panel meetings of the International Panel on the Regulation of Autonomous Weapons (IPRAW), the precautionary principle was often invoked as being applicable to the debate on autonomous weapons. As Cass

Sunstein (2005, 1) notes, '[t]he simplest interpretation of the precautionary principle is that "it is better to be safe than sorry". But the principle comes in many diverse forms, ranging from weak to strong.' Sunstein contends that 'the precautionary principle does not help individuals or nations make difficult choices in a non-arbitrary way. Taken seriously, it can be paralysing, providing no direction at all.' In this book I have outlined an approach to weighing the risks that might be imposed by the employment of autonomous weapons that, I contend, is neither paralysing nor arbitrary, but is instead consistent with core principles of liberalism, in that it pays due respect to the opposing and deep-seated moral intuitions held by a state's citizens. This approach shows, counter to the views of many engaged in the debate over autonomous weapons, that the issue of human dignity does not necessarily 'trump' all other considerations. The key question is instead whether autonomous weapons can be applied in a way that reduces the risk of death or harm to non-combatants and own forces. Given that there are good reasons to believe that this is in fact feasible, I conclude that we should *not* ban 'killer robots'.

References

Baker, Deane-Peter. 2011. *Just Warriors, Inc: The Ethics of Privatized Force*. Continuum.

Baker, Deane-Peter. 2016. *Citizen Killings: Liberalism, State Policy and Moral Risk*. Bloomsbury Academic.

Baker, Deane-Peter. forthcoming. 'Exploring western and Chinese responses to the ethical challenge of lethal autonomous weapons', in *The Ethical Implications of Emerging Technologies in Warfare*, edited by Bernhard Koch and Richard Schoonhoven. Martinus Nijhoff/Brill.

Barry, Christian and Lars Christie. 2018. 'The moral equality of combatants', in *The Oxford Handbook of Ethics and War*, edited by Seth Lazar and Helen Frowe. Oxford University Press. DOI: 10.1093/oxfordhb/9780199943418.013.28.

Coady, C. A. J. 1992. 'Mercenary morality', in *International Law and Armed Conflict*, edited by A. G. D. Bradney. Steiner, pp. 55–69.

Coates, A. J. 1997. *The Ethics of War*. Manchester University Press.

Dennett, Daniel. 1984. *Elbow Room: The Varieties of Free Will Worth Wanting*. MIT Press.

Devitt, S. Kate. 2018. 'Trustworthiness in autonomous systems', in *Foundations of Trusted Autonomy*, edited by Hussein A. Abbas, Jason Scholz and Darryn J. Reid. Springer Open, pp. 161–84.

Feaver, Peter D. 2003. *Armed Servants: Agency, Oversight, and Civil–Military Relations*. Harvard University Press.

Foster, E. S. 1941. 'Dogs in ancient warfare'. *Greece & Rome* 10: 114–17.

Future of Life Institute. n.d. 'Lethal autonomous weapons pledge'. https://futureoflife.org/lethal-autonomous-weapons-pledge/?cn-reloaded=1.

Holy See. 2015. Statement of the Holy See, CCW Meeting of Experts on Lethal Autonomous Weapons Systems, Geneva, 16 April.

Horowitz, Michael C. 2016. 'Public opinion and the politics of the killer robots debate'. *Research & Politics* 3(1): 1–8.

Human Rights Watch. 2016. 'Killer robots and the concept of meaningful human control'. https://www.hrw.org/news/2016/04/11/killer-robots-and-concept-meaningful-human-control.

Huntington, Samuel. 1957. *The Soldier and the State*. Harvard University Press.

ICRC. 2016. 'Autonomous weapon systems: Implications of increasing autonomy in the critical functions of weapons'. 1 September. https://www.icrc.org/en/publication/4283-autonomous-weapons-systems.

ICRC. 2018. 'Ethics and autonomous weapon systems:

An ethical basis for human control?' Geneva, 3 April 2018.

ICRC. 2021. 'ICRC position on autonomous weapon systems'. Geneva, 12 May 2021. https://www.icrc.org/en/document/icrc-position-autonomous-weapon-systems.

IPRAW. n.d. 'Welcome'. www.ipraw.org.

Kania, Elsa B. 2017. *Battlefield Singularity: Artificial Intelligence, Military Revolution, and China's Future Military Power*. Center for a New American Security.

Lewis, Michael, Katia Sycara and Phillip Walker. 2018. 'The role of trust in human-robot interaction', in *Foundations of Trusted Autonomy*, edited by Hussein A. Abbas, Jason Scholz and Darryn J. Reid. Springer Open, pp. 135–59.

Lynch, Tony and A. J. Walsh. 2000. The good mercenary? *Journal of Political Philosophy* 8(2): 133–53.

Madrigal, Alexis C. 2011. 'Old, weird tech: The bat bombs of World War II'. *The Atlantic*, 14 April.

Martin, George. 2018. 'Hero SAS dog saves the lives of six elite soldiers by ripping out jihadi's throat while taking down three terrorists who ambushed British patrol'. *Daily Mail*, 8 July.

Matson, Mike. 2018. 'Demons in the long grass'. Mad Scientist Laboratory [blog], 19 June. https://madsciblog.tradoc.army.mil/tag/demons-in-the-grass.

Matson, Mike. n.d. 'Demons in the long grass'. *Small Wars Journal: Blog Posts*. http://smallwarsjournal.com/jrnl/art/demons-tall-grass.

McGowan, Patrick J. 2003. 'African military coups

d'état, 1956–2001: Frequency, trends and distribution'. *Journal of Modern African Studies* 41(3): 339–70.

Morkevičius, Valerie. 2018. *Realist Ethics: Just War Traditions as Power Politics*. Cambridge University Press.

Norton-Taylor, Richard. 2010. 'SAS parachute dogs of war into Taliban bases'. *Guardian*, 8 November.

Pattison, James. 2010. *Humanitarian Intervention and the Responsibility to Protect: Who Should Intervene?* Oxford University Press.

Santoni de Sio, Filippo and Jerome van den Hoven. 2018. 'Meaningful human control over autonomous systems: A philosophical account'. *Frontiers in Robotics and AI* 5, 28 February. https://doi.org/10.3389/frobt.2018.00015.

Scharre, Paul. 2018. *Army of None: Autonomous Weapons and the Future of War*. Norton.

Singer, Peter W. 2003. *Corporate Warriors: The Rise of the Privatized Military Industry*. Cornell University Press.

Skerker, Michael, Duncan Purves and Ryan Jenkins. 2020. 'Autonomous weapons systems and the moral equality of combatants'. *Ethics and Information Technology* 22: 197–209. https://doi.org/10.1007/s10676-020-09528-0.

Skinner, B. F. 1960. 'Pigeons in a pelican'. *American Psychologist*, 15(1): 28–37.

Steingart, Gabor. 2009. 'Memo reveals details of Blackwater targeted killings program'. *Der Spiegel*, 24 August.

Sugg, Stewart. 2017. *Slaughterbots* [film]. Space Digital. Released 12 November.

Sunstein, Cass R. 2005. 'The precautionary principle as a basis for decision making', *Economists' Voice* 2(2): 1–10.

Taylor, Charles. 1989. *Sources of the Self: The Making of the Modern Identity*. Harvard University Press.

Taylor, Charles. 2004. *Modern Social Imaginaries*. Duke University Press.

Taylor, Charles. 2007. *A Secular Age*. Harvard University Press.

Townsend, Mark. 2005. 'Armed and dangerous: Flipper the firing dolphin let loose by Katrina'. *Observer*, 25 September.

UN. 2016. 'Joint report of the UN special rapporteur on the rights to freedom of peaceful assembly and of association and the UN special rapporteur on extrajudicial, summary or arbitrary executions on the proper management of assemblies, to the Human Rights Council'. A/HRC/31/66, 4 February. https://www. refworld.org/docid/575135464.html.

US Army CCDC Army Research Laboratory Public Affairs. 2020. 'Augmented Reality K9 Goggles could help protect soldiers' [press release]. 10 July. https:// soldiersystems.net/2020/10/07/augmented-reality-k9-goggles-could-help-protect-soldiers.

Vincent, James. 2019. 'Former Go champion beaten by DeepMind retires after declaring AI invincible'. *The Verge*, 27 November. https://www.theverge.com/2019/ 11/27/20985260/ai-go-alphago-lee-se-dol-retired-deep mind-defeat.